The Master's Indwelling

There is a life of abundance and joy!

Other Titles by Andrew Murray

Abide in Christ
Absolute Surrender
Andrew Murray Devotional
Andrew Murray on Prayer
Andrew Murray on the Holy Spirit
The Blessings of Obedience
The Blood of the Cross
Covenants and Blessings
Daily Experience with God
The Deeper Christian Life
An Exciting New Life
Experiencing the Holy Spirit
Full Life in Christ
God's Best Secrets
God's Plans for You
God's Power for Today
God's Will: Our Dwelling Place
Healing Secrets (Divine Healing)
The Holiest of All
How to Strengthen Your Faith
Humility
The Minstry of Intercession
The Power of the Blood of Christ
The Practice of God's Presence
Prayer Power
Raising Your Children for Christ
The Secret of God's Presence
The Secret of Intercession
The Secret of Spiritual Strength
Secrets of Authority
The True Vine
Waiting on God
With Christ in the School of Prayer

The Master's Indwelling

There is a life of abundance and joy!

Andrew Murray

Whitaker House

All Scripture quotations are taken from the King James Version (KJV) of the Bible.

Publisher's note:
This new edition from Whitaker House has been updated for the modern reader. Words, expressions, and sentence structure have been revised for clarity and readability.

THE MASTER'S INDWELLING

ISBN-13: 978-0-88368-843-4
ISBN-10: 0-88368-843-3
Printed in the United States of America

WHITAKER HOUSE
1030 Hunt Valley Circle
New Kensington, PA 15068
www.whitakerhouse.com

Library of Congress Cataloging-in-Publication Data

Murray, Andrew, 1828–1917.
Master's indwelling / by Andrew Murray.
p. cm.
Edited for the modern reader. Words, expressions, and sentence structure have been updated for clarity and readability.
ISBN 0-88368-843-3 (pbk.)
1. Christian life. I. Title.
BV4501.3 .M89 2002
248.4—dc21
2002012325

2 3 4 5 6 7 8 9 10 W 12 11 10 09 08 07

Contents

Chapter One

Carnal Christians

Chapter One

Carnal Christians

"And I, brethren, could not speak unto you as unto spiritual, but as unto carnal."
—1 Corinthians 3:1

Here the apostle spoke about two stages of Christian life—two types of Christians—spiritual and carnal. The Corinthians were Christians; they were in Christ. But, instead of being spiritual Christians, they were carnal. *"I have fed you with milk, and not with meat: for hitherto ye were not able to bear it, neither yet now are ye able. For ye are yet carnal"* (1 Corinthians 3:2–3). Here is that word a second time. *"For whereas"*—in other words, "this is the proof"—*"there is among you envying, and strife, and divisions, are ye not carnal, and walk as men? For while one saith, I am of Paul; and another, I am of Apollos; are ye not carnal?"* (I Corinthians 3:3–4).

Four times the apostle used the word *carnal.* In the wisdom that the Holy Spirit gave him, Paul felt this: "I cannot write to these Corinthian Christians unless I know their state and unless I tell them of it. If I give spiritual food to men who are carnal Christians, I am doing them more harm than good, for they are not fit to take it. I cannot feed them with meat; I must feed them with milk." And so he told them at the very outset of the epistle what he believed their state to be. In the two previous chapters, he had spoken about his ministry being by the Holy Spirit. Now he began to tell them what state people must have in order to accept spiritual truth, and he said, "I cannot speak to you as I would like, for you are carnal and cannot receive spiritual truth." That suggests to us the solemn thought that, in the church, there are two classes of Christians.

Two Classes of Christians

Some have lived many years as believers yet they always remain babes; others are spiritual men because they have given themselves up to the power, the leading, and the entire rule of the Holy Spirit. If we are to obtain a blessing, we must first decide to which of these classes we belong. Are we, by the grace of God, living a spiritual life in deep humility, or are we living a carnal life? Let us try to understand what is meant by the carnal state in which believers may be living.

Marks of the Carnal State

We notice, from what we find in 1 Corinthians, that there are four marks of the carnal state. First, it is simply a condition of protracted infancy. Let me illustrate what that means. Imagine a beautiful baby, six months old. He cannot speak; he cannot walk. But we do not trouble ourselves about that. This is natural and ought to be so. But suppose a year later we find the child not grown at all, and three years later, still no growth. We would at once say, "There must be some terrible disease." And the baby, who at six months old was the cause of joy to everyone who saw him, has become a source of anxiety and sorrow. There is something wrong; the child cannot grow. It was quite right at six months old that he would eat nothing but milk. But years have passed, and he remains in the same weak state.

Now this is the condition of many believers. They are converted; they know what it is to have assurance and faith; they believe in pardon for sin; they begin to work for God. Yet, somehow, there is very little growth in their spirituality, in the real heavenly life. We come into contact with them, and we at once feel that there is something missing. There is none of the beauty of holiness or the power of God's Spirit in them. This is the condition of the carnal Corinthians, expressed in what was said to the Hebrews: *"For when for the time ye ought to be teachers, ye have need that one teach you again which be the first principles of the oracles of God"* (Hebrews 5:12). Is it not a sad thing to see a believer who has been converted for five, ten, or twenty years, yet has no growth, no strength, and no joy of holiness?

What are the marks of a little child? One is that a little child cannot help himself but is always keeping others occupied with serving him. What a tyrant a baby often is in a household! The mother cannot go out, for she must be there to nurse him; he needs to be cared for constantly. God made man to care for others, but the baby was made to be cared for and to be helped. Likewise, there are Christians who always want help. Their pastor and their Christian friends must always be teaching and comforting them. They go to church, to prayer meetings, and to conventions, always wanting to be helped—a sign of spiritual infancy.

The Master's Indwelling

The other sign of an infant is this: He can do nothing to help his fellowman. Every man is expected to contribute something to the welfare of society. Everyone has a place to fill and a work to do. But the babe can do nothing for the common good. It is just so with Christians. How little some can do! They take part in work, as it is called, but they exercise little of the spiritual power or the carrying of real blessing. We each should ask, "Have I outgrown my spiritual infancy?" Some must reply, "No, instead of having gone forward, I have gone backward, and the joy of conversion and the first love is gone." Alas, they are babes in Christ; they are still carnal.

Continual Sin and Failure

The second mark of the carnal state is this: There is continual sin and failure. Paul said, *"For whereas there is among you envying, and strife, and divisions, are ye not carnal?"* A man gives way to temper. He may be a minister, a preacher of the Gospel, or a Sunday school teacher—most earnest at the prayer meeting—yet he often shows strife, bitterness, or envy. Alas, in Galatians 5:20–21, we are told that the works of the flesh are characterized especially by hatred and envy. How often we see divisions and bitterness among Christians who have to work together!

God have mercy upon them so that the fruit of the Spirit, love, will not be so frequently absent from His own people.

You ask, "Why is it that for twenty years I have been fighting with my temper and cannot conquer it?" It is because you have been fighting with the temper, and you have not been fighting with the root of the temper. You have not seen that it is because you are in the carnal state, not properly given up to the Spirit of God. It may be that you never were taught it, that you never saw it in God's Word, or that you never believed it. But there it is; the truth of God remains unchangeable. Jesus Christ can give us the victory over sin and can keep us from actual transgression. I am not telling you that the root of sin will be eradicated and that you will no longer have any natural tendency to sin. But when the Holy Spirit comes, not only with His power for service as a gift but also with divine grace to fill the heart, there is victory over sin. There is power to resist the lusts of the flesh.

We see a mark of the carnal state not only in unlovingness, self-consciousness, and bitterness, but also in so many other sins. How much worldliness, ambition among men, and seeking for the honor that comes from man—all the fruit of the carnal life—may be found in the midst of Christian activity! Let us remember that the carnal state is a state of continual sinning and failure. God wants us not only to make confession of individual sins but also to acknowledge that they are the sign that we are not living a healthy life—that we are yet carnal.

A Difference between Grace and Gifts

A third mark that will further explain what I have been saying is that this carnal state may co-eixst with spiritual gifts. There is a difference between gifts and graces. The graces of the Spirit are humility and love, like the humility and love of Christ. The graces of the Spirit are to make a man free from self. The gifts of the Spirit are to fit a man for work. We see this illustrated among the Corinthians. In the first chapter, Paul said, *"I thank my God... that in every thing ye are enriched by him, in all utterance, and in all knowledge"* (1 Corinthians 1:4–5). In the twelfth and fourteenth chapters, we see that the gifts of prophecy and of working miracles were in great power among them. But the graces of the Spirit were noticeably absent.

This may occur in our day as well, as it did in the time of the Corinthians. I may be a minister of the Gospel; I may teach God's Word beautifully; I may have influence and gather a large congregation, yet, alas, I may be a carnal man. I may be a man who is used by God, a blessing to others, yet the carnal life may still mark me. You all know the law that a thing is named according to its most prominent characteristic. Now in these carnal Corinthians there was a little of God's Spirit, but the flesh predominated. The Spirit did not have rule of their whole lives. And spiritual men are not called so because there is no flesh in them, but because the Spirit in them has obtained dominance. When you meet them and have fellowship with them, you feel that the Spirit of God has sanctified them. Ah, let us beware of allowing the blessing God gives us in our work to deceive us and lead us to think that, because He has blessed us, we are certainly spiritual men. God may give us gifts that we use, yet our lives may not be wholly in the power of the Holy Spirit.

Unfit for Spiritual Truths

The last mark of the carnal state is that it makes a man unfit for receiving spiritual truths. That is essentially what the apostle wrote to the Corinthians: "I could not preach to you as unto the spiritual. You are not fit for spiritual truth after being Christians so long; you cannot yet bear it. I have to feed you with milk." I am afraid that the church of today often makes a terrible mistake. The majority of people in our congregations are carnal. We give them spiritual teaching, and they admire it, understand it, and rejoice in such ministry. Yet their lives are not practically affected. They work for Christ in a certain way, but we can barely recognize the true sanctification of the Spirit. We dare not say they are spiritual people, full of the Holy Spirit.

Now let us recognize this with regard to ourselves. A man may become very earnest and may take in all the teaching he hears. He may be able to discern, for discernment is a gift. He may say, "That man helps me in this line, and that man in another direction, and a third man is remarkable for another gift." Yet, all the time, the carnal life may be living strongly in him, and when he gets into trouble with some friends, a Christian worker, or a worldly man, the carnal root grows and bears its terrible fruit because he has failed to allow spiritual food to enter his heart. Beware of that. Mark the Corinthians and learn from them. Paul did not say to them, "You cannot bear the truth as I would speak it to you," because they were ignorant or stupid people. The Corinthians prided themselves on their wisdom and sought it above everything. Notice that Paul said, in essence, "I thank God that you are enriched in utterance, in knowledge, and in wisdom; nevertheless, you are yet carnal; your life is not holy. Your life is not sanctified unto the humility of the life of the Lamb of God; you cannot yet take in real spiritual truth." (See 1 Corinthians 1–3.)

We find the carnal state not only at Corinth but also throughout the Christian world today. Many Christians are asking, "Why is there so much feebleness in the church?" We cannot ask this question too earnestly, and I trust that God Himself will so impress it upon our hearts that we will say to Him, "It must be changed. Have mercy on us." But, ah, that prayer and that change cannot come until we have begun to see that there is a carnal root ruling in believers. They are living more after the flesh than the Spirit. They are yet carnal Christians.

There is a passing from carnal into spiritual. Did Paul find any spiritual believers? Undoubtedly he did. Read chapter six of the epistle to the Galatians. That was a church where strife, bitterness, and envy were rampant. But the apostle said in the first verse, *"Brethren, if a man be overtaken in a fault, ye which are spiritual, restore such an one in the spirit of meekness."* There we see that the marks of the spiritual man are that he will be a meek man. He will have power and love to help and restore those who have fallen. The carnal man cannot do that. If there is a true spiritual life that can be lived, the great question is this: Is the way open, and how can I enter into the spiritual state? Here, again, I have four short answers.

How to Enter the Spiritual State

1. *We must know that there is such a spiritual life to be lived by men on earth.* Nothing severs the roots of the Christian life as much as unbelief. People do not believe what God has said about what He is willing to do for His children. Men do not believe that when God says, *"Be filled with the Spirit,"* He means it for every Christian. Yet Paul wrote to the Ephesians, each one, *"And be not drunk with wine, wherein is excess; but be filled with the Spirit"* (Ephesians 5:18). Just as little as you may be drunk with wine, so little may you live without being filled with the Spirit. Now if God intends this for believers, the first thing that we must do is study and take home God's Word until our hearts are filled with the assurance that there is such a spiritual life. And it is our duty to live that life. We can be spiritual men. God's Word teaches us that God does not expect a man to live as he ought for one minute without the Holy Spirit enabling him to do it.

We do not want the Holy Spirit only when we go to preach or when we have some special temptation of the devil to meet—some great burden to bear. God said, "My child cannot live a right life unless he is guided by My Spirit every minute." That is the mark of the child of God: *"For as many as are led by the Spirit of God, they are the sons of God"* (Romans 8:14). In Romans, we read, *"The love of God is shed abroad in our hearts by the Holy Ghost which is given unto us"* (Romans 5:5). That is to be the common, everyday experience of the believer, not only at certain times. Did a father or mother ever think, "Just for today, I want my child to love me?" No, they expect love every day.

And so God wants His child to always have a heart filled with love of the Spirit. In the eyes of God, it is most unnatural to expect a man to love as he should if he is not filled with the Spirit. Oh, let us believe a man can be a spiritual man. Thank God, the blessing is now waiting for us. *"Be filled with the Spirit."* Be led by the Spirit. There is the blessing. If you have to say, "O God, I do not have this blessing," say it. But also say, "Lord, I know it is my duty, my solemn obligation to have it, for without it I cannot live in perfect peace with You all the day. Without it I cannot glorify You and do the work You would have me do." This is our first step from carnal to spiritual—to recognize that a spiritual life, a walk in the Spirit, is within our reach. How can we ask God to guide us into a spiritual life if we do not have a clear, confident conviction that there is such a life to be had?

2. *A man must see the shame and guilt of his having lived such a carnal life.* Some people admit there is a spiritual life to live, acknowledge that they have not lived it, and then feel sorry for themselves. They pity themselves and think, "How sad that I am too feeble for it! How sad that God gives it to others but has not given it to me!" They have great compassion for themselves, instead of saying, "Alas, it has been my unfaithfulness, unbelief, and disobedience that has kept me from giving myself utterly to God. I must blush and be ashamed before God that I do not live as a spiritual man."

A man is not converted without first having a conviction of sin. When that conviction of sin comes and his eyes are opened, he learns to be afraid of his sin. He learns to flee from it to Christ and to accept Christ as a mighty deliverer. But a man needs a second conviction of sin; a believer must be convicted of his particular sins. The sins of an unconverted man are different from the sins of a believer. An unconverted man, for instance, is not ordinarily convicted of the corruption of his nature; he thinks principally about external sins—"I have sworn, been a liar, and I am on the way to hell." He is then convicted for conversion.

But the believer is in quite a different condition. His sins are far more blameable, for he has had the light and the love and the Spirit of God given to him. His sins are far deeper. He has striven to conquer them and he has grown to see that his nature is utterly corrupt. The carnal mind, the flesh within him, makes his whole state utterly wretched. When a believer is thus convicted by the Holy Spirit, his life of unbelief especially condemns him because he sees that the great guilt connected with this has kept him from receiving the full gift of God's Holy Spirit. He is brought down in shame and confusion of face. He begins to cry, "Woe is me, for I am undone. I have heard of God. I have known a great deal of Him and preached about Him, but now my eyes see Him." God comes near to him. Job, the righteous man whom God allowed to be tested, saw in himself the deep sin of self-righteousness, which he had never seen before. Until this conviction of the wrongness of our carnal state as believers comes, until we are willing to get this conviction from God—to take time before God to be humbled and convicted—we can never become spiritual men.

3. *Going out of the carnal state into the spiritual is only one step.* One step. Oh, that is a blessed message I bring to you—it is only one step. I know many people will refuse to admit that it is only one step. They think too little for such a mighty change. But was not conversion only one step?

So it is when a man passes from carnal to spiritual. You ask if, when I speak of a spiritual man, I am thinking of a man of spiritual maturity, a real saint, and you say, "Does that come in one day? Is there no growth in holiness?" I reply that spiritual maturity cannot come in a day. We cannot expect it. It takes time for the whole beauty of the image of Christ to be formed in a man. But I still say that it only takes one step for a man to get out of the carnal life into the spiritual life. It is when a man utterly breaks with the flesh, when he gives up the flesh into the crucifixion death of Christ, that he understands how to enter the spiritual life. When he sees that everything about his carnal life is accursed, that he cannot deliver himself from it, and thus claims the slaying power of Christ's cross within him, then he turns to Christ and begs forgiveness.

When a man does this and says, "This spiritual life prepared for me is the free gift of my God in Christ Jesus," he understands how one step can bring him out of the carnal into the spiritual state.

In that spiritual life, there will still be much to learn. There will still be imperfections. Spiritual life is not perfect. But the predominant characteristic will be spiritual. When a man has given himself up to the real, living, acting, ruling power of God's Spirit, he has discovered the right position in which he can grow. You never think of growing out of sickness into health. You may grow out of feebleness into strength, as the little babe can grow to be a strong man. But where there is disease, healing must come if there is to be a cure. There are Christians who think that they must grow out of the carnal state into the spiritual state. You never can. What could help those carnal Corinthians? To give them milk will not help them, for milk is a proof they are in the wrong state. To give them meat will not help them, for they are unfit to eat it. What they need is the knife of the surgeon. Paul said that the carnal life must be cut out. *"They that are Christ's have crucified the flesh with the affections and lusts"* (Galatians 5:24).

When a man understands what that means and accepts it in the faith of what Christ can do, then one step can bring him from carnal to spiritual. One simple act of faith in the power of Christ's death, one act of surrender to the fellowship of Christ's death in the Holy Spirit, can make it ours, will make it ours. It will bring deliverance from the power of our efforts.

What brought deliverance to that poor condemned sinner who was most dark and wretched in his unconverted state? He felt he could do nothing good by himself. What did he do? He saw before him the almighty Savior and he cast himself into His arms. He trusted himself to that omnipotent love and cried, "Lord, have mercy upon me." That was salvation. It was not for what he did that Christ accepted him. Believers, if any who are conscious that the carnal state predominates—if any say, "It marks me. I am a religious man, an earnest man, a friend of missions. I work for Christ in my church, but alas, temper and sin and worldliness still master my soul"—hear the Word of God.

If any come and say, "I have struggled, prayed, and wept, and it has not helped me," then you must do one other thing. You must see that the living Christ is God's provision for your holy, spiritual life. You must believe that Christ, who accepted you once at conversion, in His wonderful love, is now waiting to say that you may become a spiritual man, entirely given up to God. If you will believe that, your fear will vanish and you will say, "It can be done. If Christ will accept and take charge, it will be done."

4. *A man must take that step, a solemn but blessed step.* It took some of you five or ten years before you took the step of conversion. You wept and prayed for years and could not find peace until you took that step. Likewise, in the spiritual life, you may go to teacher after teacher and say, "Tell me about the spiritual life, the baptism of the Spirit, and holiness," yet you may remain just where you were. Many of us would love to have sin taken away. Who loves to have a hasty temper? Who loves to have a proud disposition? Who loves to have a worldly heart? No one. We go to Christ to take it away, and He does not do it. We ask, "Why will He not do it? I have prayed very earnestly." It is because you wanted Him to take away the ugly fruits while the poisonous root was to stay in you. You did not ask Him for your flesh to be nailed to His cross. You did not say that you would henceforth give up self entirely to the power of His Spirit.

There is deliverance, but not in the way we seek it. Suppose a painter has a piece of canvas on which he desired to work out some beautiful picture. Suppose that piece of canvas does not belong to him, and anyone has a right to take it and use it for any other purpose. Do you think the painter would put much work into that canvas? No. Yet people want Jesus Christ to give His time in taking away this temper or that other sin, though in their hearts they have not yielded themselves utterly to His command and His keeping. It cannot be. But if you will come and give your whole life into His charge, Christ Jesus is mighty to save. Christ Jesus waits to be gracious. Christ Jesus waits to fill you with His Spirit.

Encouragement for Spiritual Life

Will you not take the step? God grant that we may be led by His Spirit to a yielding up of ourselves to Him as never before. Will you not come in humble confession that the carnal life has predominated too much, has altogether marked you? Confess that you have a bitter consciousness that, with all the blessing God has bestowed, you are not yet what you want to be—a spiritual man. It is the Holy Spirit alone who, by His indwelling, can make a spiritual man. Come then and cast yourself at God's feet with this one thought: "Lord, I give myself as an empty vessel to be filled with Your Spirit."

Each one of you has seen an empty tea cup sit there, waiting to be filled with tea when the proper time comes. The same goes for every dish, every plate. They are clean and empty, ready to be filled. Emptied and cleansed. Oh, come, and, just as a vessel is set apart to receive what it is to contain, say to Christ that you desire, from this time forward, to be a vessel set apart to be filled with His Spirit, given up to be a spiritual man. Bow down in the deepest emptiness of soul and say, "O God, I have nothing!" Then as surely as you place yourself before Him, you have a right to say, "My God will fulfill His promise! I claim from Him the filling of the Holy Spirit to make me, not a carnal but a spiritual Christian." If you place yourself at His feet and tarry there—if you abide in that humble surrender and that childlike trust—as sure as God lives, the blessing will come.

Oh, we must bow in shame before God as we think of His whole church and see so much of the carnal prevailing. We must bow in shame before God as we think of so much of the carnal in our hearts and lives. Then let us bow in great faith in God's mercy. Deliverance is nigh; deliverance is coming; deliverance is waiting; deliverance is sure. Let us trust. God will give it.

Chapter Two

The Self-Life

Chapter Two

The Self-Life

"If any man will come after me, let him deny himself, and take up his cross, and follow me."
—Matthew 16:24

We read that Jesus at Caesarea Philippi asked His disciples, *"Whom do men say that I the Son of man am?"* (Matthew 16:13). When they had answered, He asked them, *"But whom say ye that I am?"* (verse 15). And Peter answered, *"Thou art the Christ, the Son of the living God"* (verse 16). Jesus answered him:

> *Blessed art thou, Simon Barjona: for flesh and blood hath not revealed it unto thee, but my Father which is in heaven. And I say also unto thee, That thou art Peter, and upon this rock I will build my church; and the gates of hell shall not prevail against it."* (Matthew 16: 17–18)

Then we read how Jesus began to tell His disciples of His approaching death, and Peter began to rebuke Him saying, *"Be it far from thee, Lord: this shall not be unto thee"* (verse 22). But Jesus turned and said to Peter, *"Get thee behind me, Satan: thou art an offence unto me: for thou savourest not the things that be of God, but those that be of men"* (verse 23). Then Jesus said to His disciples, *"If any man will come after me, let him deny himself, and take up his cross, and follow me"* (verse 24).

We often hear about people who compromise their lives, and we wonder what lies at the root of it. Why do so many Christians waste their lives in the terrible bondage of the world instead of living in the manifestation, the privilege, and the glory of the child of God? And another question perhaps comes to us: Why, when we see a thing is wrong and strive against it, can we not conquer it? Why have we prayed and vowed a hundred times, yet still live a mingled, divided, half-hearted life?

The Root of the Trouble

To those two questions, there is one answer: It is self that is the root of the whole trouble. And, therefore, if anyone asks me, "How can I get rid of this compromised life?", the answer would not be, "You must do this, or that, or the other thing." The answer must be, "A new life from above, the life of Christ, must take the place of the self-life. Only then can we be conquerors."

We always go from the outward to the inward; let us do so here. Let us consider from these words of the text the one word *"self."* Jesus said to Peter, *"If any man will come after me, let him deny himself* [his own self], *and take up his cross, and follow me."* That is a mark of the true disciple. That is the secret of the Christian life—deny self and all will come right. Note that Peter was a believer—a believer who had been taught by the Holy Spirit. He had given an answer that pleased Christ wonderfully. *"Thou art the Christ, the Son of the living God."* Do not think that that was nothing extraordinary. We learn it in our catechisms; Peter did not. Christ saw that the Holy Spirit of the Father had been teaching Peter and He said, *"Blessed art thou, Simon Barjona."*

But note how strong the carnal man still was in Peter. Christ spoke of His cross, and Peter could understand about the glory, *"Thou art the Son of God."* But he could not understand the death, and he ventured in his self-confidence to say, essentially, "Lord, that will never be. You cannot be crucified and die." And Christ had to rebuke him: *"Get thee behind me, Satan...for thou savourest not the things that be of God, but those that be of men."* Peter was talking like a mere carnal man and not as the Spirit of God would teach him. Then Christ went on to say, in essence, "Remember, it is not only I who am to be crucified but you as well. It is not only I who am to die but you also. If a man wants to be My disciple, he must deny self, take up his cross, and follow Me." Let us dwell on this one word, *"self."* It is only once we learn what self is that we know the root of all our failure and are prepared to go to Christ for deliverance.

The Nature of the Self-life

Let us consider, first of all, the nature of this self-life. Then we will denote some of its works and ask the question: "How may we be delivered from it?"

Self is the power with which God has created and endowed every intelligent being. Self is the very center of a created being. And why did God give the angels and man a self? The object of this self was that it might be an empty vessel for God, that He might put His life into it as we brought it to Him. God gave me the power of self-determination so that I might bring this self to Him every day and say, "O

God, work in it. I offer it to You." God wanted a vessel into which He might pour out His divine fullness of beauty, wisdom, and power. And so He created the world, the sun, the moon, the stars, the trees, the flowers, and the grass, which all show forth the riches of His wisdom, beauty, and goodness. But they do it without knowing what they do.

Then God created the angels with a self and a will, to see whether they would come and voluntarily yield themselves to Him as vessels for Him to fill. But, alas, they did not all do that. There was one at the head of a great company who began to look on himself, thinking of the wonderful powers with which God had endowed him, and delight in himself. He began to think, "Must such a being as I always remain dependent on God?" He exalted himself, pride asserted itself in separation from God; at that very moment he became, instead of an angel in heaven, a devil in hell. Self turned to God is the glory of allowing the Creator to reveal Himself in us. Self turned away from God is the very darkness and fire of hell.

We all know the terrible story that took place after that—God created man, and Satan came in the form of a serpent to tempt Eve with the thought of becoming like God, having an independent self, knowing good and evil. And while he spoke with her, he breathed into her with his words the very poison and pride of hell. His own evil spirit, the very poison of hell, entered humanity, and it is this cursed self that we have inherited from our first parents. It was that self that ruined and brought destruction upon this world, as well as all that there has been of sin, darkness, wretchedness, and misery. And all that there will be throughout the countless ages of eternity in hell will be nothing but the reign of self, the curse of self, separating man and turning him away from his God. And if we are to fully understand what Christ is to do for us and are to become partakers of a full salvation, we must learn to know, to hate, and to entirely give up this cursed self.

The Works of Self

Now what are the works of self? I might mention many, but let us take the simplest words that we are continually using—*self-will, self-confidence, self-exaltation. Self-will,* pleasing self, is the great sin of man; it is at the root of all compromising to the world, which is the ruin of so many. Men cannot understand why they should not please themselves and do their own wills. Numbers of Christians have never understood the idea that a Christian is a man who never seeks his own will but is always seeking the will of God. He is a man in whom the very spirit of Christ lives. *"Lo, I come to do thy will, O God"* (Hebrews 10:9)!

We find Christians pleasing themselves in a thousand ways and yet trying to be happy, good, and useful. They do not know that self-will is at the root of it all, robbing them of the blessing. Christ said to Peter, "Peter, deny yourself." But instead of doing that, Peter said through his actions, "I will deny my Lord and not myself." Christ had said to him the night before, *"Thou shalt deny me"* (Matthew 26:34), and Peter did it.

What was the cause of this? *Self-will.* Peter became afraid when the woman servant charged him with belonging to Jesus, and three times he said, *"I know not the man"* (Matthew 26:74). He denied Christ. Just think of it! It was a choice between self—that ugly, cursed self—and the beautiful, blessed Son of God. Peter chose self. No wonder he thought, "Instead of denying myself, I have denied Jesus. What a choice I have made!" No wonder he wept bitterly.

Christians, look at your own lives in the light of the words of Jesus. Do you find self-will and self-pleasing there? Remember this—every time you please yourself, you deny Jesus. It is one or the other. You must please only Him and deny self, or you must please yourself and deny Him. Then follows self-confidence, self-trust, self-effort, and self-dependence. What was it that led Peter to deny Jesus? Christ had warned him; why did he not take warning? *Self-confidence.* He was so sure: "Lord, I love You. For three years I have followed You. Lord, I deny that it ever can be. I am ready to go to prison and to death." It was simply self-confidence.

People have often asked me, "Why do I fail? I desire so earnestly, and pray so fervently, to live in God's will." And my answer generally is, "Simply because you trust yourself." They answer, "No, I do not. I know I am not good. I know that God is willing to keep me, and I put my trust in Jesus." But I reply, "No, my brother, no. If you trusted God and Jesus, you could not fail, but you trust yourself." Do let us believe that the cause of every failure in the Christian life is nothing but this: I trust this cursed self, instead of trusting Jesus. I trust my own strength, instead of the almighty strength of God. And that is why Christ says, "This self must be denied."

Then there is *self-exaltation,* another form of the works of self. Ah, how much pride and jealousy there is in the Christian world. How much sensitiveness to what men say of us or think of us. How much desire of human praise and pleasing men, instead of always living in the presence of God with the one thought: "Am I pleasing to Him?" Christ said, *"How can ye believe, which receive honour one of another?"* (John 5:44). Receiving honor of one another renders a life of faith absolutely impossible. This self started from hell, separated us from God, and is a cursed deceiver that leads us astray from Jesus.

What are we to do to get rid of this self-life? Jesus answers us in the words of our text: *"If any man will come after me, let him deny himself, and take up his cross, and follow me."* Note it well: I must deny myself and take Jesus Himself as my life; I must choose. There are two lives, the self-life and the Christ-life; I must choose one of the two. "Follow Me," says our Lord. "Make Me the law of your existence, the rule of your conduct. Give Me your whole heart. Follow Me, and I will care for all." O friends, it is a solemn exchange to have set before us. How wonderful to come and, seeing the danger of this self with its pride and its wickedness, to cast ourselves before the Son of God and to say, "I deny my own life; I take Your life to be mine."

Denying Self

The reason Christians pray and pray without results for the Christ-life to come into them is that the self-life is not denied. You ask, "How can I get rid of this self-life?" You know the parable: The strong man kept his house until one stronger than he came in and cast him out. Then the place was swept, but empty, and the strong man came back with seven other spirits worse than himself. It is only Christ Himself coming in that can cast out self and keep it out. This self will abide with us to the very end.

Remember the apostle Paul. He had seen the heavenly vision, and so that he would not exalt himself, the thorn in the flesh was sent to humble him. There was a natural tendency to exalt himself, and it would have conquered him had Christ not delivered him from it by His faithful care for His loving servant. Jesus Christ is able, by His divine grace, to prevent the power of self from ever asserting itself or gaining the upper hand. Jesus Christ is willing to become the life of the soul. Jesus Christ is willing to teach us to follow Him and to have heart and life set upon Him alone, so that He will ever and always be the light of our souls. Then we come to what the apostle Paul said, *"Not I, but Christ liveth in me"* (Galatians 2:20). The two truths go together. First, *"Not I,"* then, *"but Christ liveth in me."*

Look at Peter again. Christ said to him, "Deny yourself, and follow Me." Where was he to follow? Jesus led him, even though Peter failed. And where did He lead Peter? He led him on to Gethsemane, and there Peter failed, for he slept when he ought to have been awake, watching and praying. He led him on toward Calvary, to the place where Peter denied Him. Was that Christ's leading? Praise God, it was. The Holy Spirit had not yet come in His power. Peter was yet a carnal man. The spirit was willing but not able to conquer, because the flesh was weak. What did Christ do? He led Peter on until he was broken down in utter self-abasement and humbled in the depths of sorrow. Jesus led him on, past the grave, through the Resurrection, up to Pentecost—and the Holy Spirit came. In the Holy Spirit, Christ with His divine life came, and then it was, *"Christ liveth in me."*

Set Your Heart on Christ

There is only one way of being delivered from this life of self. We must follow Christ, set our hearts upon Him, listen to His teachings, and give ourselves up every day so that He may be all to us. And by the power of Christ, the denial of self will be a blessed, unceasing reality. Never for one hour do I expect the Christian to reach a stage at which he can say, "I have no self to deny." Never for one moment will he be able to say, "I do not need to deny self." No, this fellowship with the cross of Christ will be an unceasing denial of self every hour and every moment by the grace of God.

There is no place where there is full deliverance from the power of this sinful self. We are to be crucified with Christ Jesus. We are to live with Him as those who have never been baptized into His death. Think of that! Christ had no sinful self, but He had a self that He actually gave up unto death. In Gethsemane, He said, *"I seek not mine own will, but the will of the Father which hath sent me"* (John 5:30). That sinless self He gave up unto death that He might receive it again out of the grave from God, raised up and glorified. Can we expect to go to heaven in any other way than He went? Beware! Remember that Christ descended into death and the grave, and it is in the death of self, following Jesus to the utmost, that the deliverance and the life will come.

And now what use are we to make of this lesson of the Master? The first lesson will be that we should take time and humble ourselves before God at the thought of what this self in us is. Put down to the account of the self every sin, every shortcoming, every failure, and everything that has been dishonoring to God, and say, "Lord, this is what I am." Then allow the blessed Jesus Christ to take entire control of your life in the faith that His life can be yours.

Do not think it is an easy thing to get rid of self. At a consecration meeting, it is easy to make a vow, to offer a prayer, and to perform an act of surrender. But as solemn as the death of Christ was on Calvary—His giving up of His sinless self-life to God—just as solemn must the giving up of self to death be between us and our God. The power of the death of Christ must come to work in us every day. Oh, what a contrast there is between self-willed Peter and Jesus giving up His will to God! What a contrast there is between that self-exaltation of Peter and the deep humility of the Lamb of God, meek and lowly in heart before God and man! What a contrast there is between that self-confidence of Peter and that deep dependence of Jesus upon the Father, shown when He said, *"I can of mine own self do nothing"* (John 5:30).

We are called upon to live the life of Christ, and Christ comes to live His life in us. But one thing must first take place—we must learn to hate this self and to deny it. As Peter said, when he denied Christ, *"I do not know the man"* (Matthew 26:72), so we must say, "I do not know this self," so that Christ Jesus may be all in all. Let us humble ourselves at the thought of what this self has done to us and how it has dishonored Jesus. Let us pray very fervently: "Lord, by Your light discover this self, we beseech You to disclose it to us. Open our eyes, that we may see what it has done and that it is the only hindrance that has been keeping us back."

Let us pray this fervently, and then let us wait upon God until we get away from all our pious exercises and experiences and from all our blessings. Let us get close to God with this one prayer: "Lord God, self changed an archangel into a devil and self ruined my first parents and brought them out of Paradise into darkness and misery. Self has been the ruin of my life and the cause of every failure. Oh, disclose it to me." And then comes the blessed exchange that a man is made willing and able to say, "Another will live the life for me; another will live with me; another will do all for me." Nothing else will do. Deny self; take up the cross to die with Jesus. Follow Him only. May He give us the grace to understand, to receive, and to live the Christ-life.

Chapter Three

Waiting on God

Chapter Three

Waiting on God

"My soul, wait thou only upon God; for my expectation is from him."
—Psalm 62:5

The solemn question arises, "Is the God I have—a God who is, to me, above any circumstances—nearer to me than any circumstance can be?" Beloved, have you learned to live your life believing that God is truly with you every moment, that, in the most difficult circumstances, He is always more present and nearer than anything around you? All our knowledge of God's Word will help us very little unless that is the question we seek to answer.

Why do so many of God's beloved children continually complain, "My circumstances separate me from God. My trials, my temptations, my character, my temper, my friends, my enemies—anything can come between my God and me"? Is God not able to take such possession of me that He can be nearer to me than anything in the world? Must riches or poverty, joy or sorrow, have a power over me that my God has not? No. But why, then, do God's children so often complain that their circumstances separate them from Him? There can be only one answer: They do not know their God.

Do We Know God?

If there is trouble or feebleness in the church of God, it is because of this. We do not know the God we have. That is why, in addition to the promise, *"I will be to you a God,"* the promise, *"And ye shall know that I am the LORD your God,"* is so often added (Exodus 6:7). If I know this truth—not through man's teaching, my mind, or my imagination, but in the living evidence that God gives in my heart—then I will know the wonder that the divine presence of my God will bring. My God Himself will be so beautiful and so near that I can live all my days and years a conqueror through Him who loved me. Is that not the life we need?

Again, we ask: Why is it that God's people do not know their God? And the answer is: They take anything rather than God—ministers, preaching, books, prayers, work, and efforts—any exertion of human nature, instead of waiting for God to reveal Himself. No teaching that we may get, no effort that we may put forth, can put us in possession of this blessed light of God, all in all to our souls. But still, it is attainable; it is within reach, if God will reveal Himself. That is the one necessity. I pray that each person would ask whether, in his heart, he has said and is saying every day, "I want more of God. Do not speak to me only of the beautiful truth there is in the Bible. That can not satisfy me. I want God."

In our inner Christian life, in our daily prayers, in our Christian living, in our churches, in our prayer meetings, in our fellowship, it must come to the point that God always has first place. If that is given to Him, He will take possession. Oh, if in our individual lives every eye were set upon God, upon the living God, and if every heart were crying, *"My soul thirsteth for God"* (Psalm 42:2), what power, what blessing, and what presence of the everlasting God would be revealed to us! Let me use an illustration. When a man is giving an illustrated lecture, he often uses a long pointer to indicate places on a map or chart. Do the people look at that pointer? No, it only helps to show them the place on the map. And they do not think about the pointer—it might be of fine gold, but the pointer cannot satisfy them. They want to see what the pointer points at.

And the Bible is nothing but a pointer, pointing to God. And—may I say it with reverence—Jesus Christ came to point us, to show us the way, to bring us to God. I am afraid there are many people who love Christ and who trust in Him but who fail in the one great object of His work. They have never learned to understand what the Scripture says, *"For Christ also hath once suffered for sins, the just for the unjust, that he might bring us to God, being put to death in the flesh, but quickened by the Spirit"* (1 Peter 3:18).

There is a difference between the way and the end at which I am aiming. I might be traveling amid very beautiful scenery, in the most delightful company. But if I have a home to which I want to go, all the scenery, all the company, and all the beauty and happiness around me cannot satisfy me. I want to reach the end. I want my home. And God is meant to be the home of our souls. Christ came into the world to bring us back to God, and unless we take Christ as God intended, our faith will always be a divided one. We read in Hebrews, chapter seven, *"He is able also to save them to the uttermost."* Whom? Those *"that come unto God by him"* (verse 25), not those who only come to Christ. In Christ—bless His name—we have the graciousness, the condescension, and the tenderness of God. But we are in danger of standing there and being content with that. Christ wants to bring us back to rejoice as much as possible in the glory of God Himself—in His righteousness, His holiness, His authority, His presence, and His power. He can completely save those who come to God through Him!

How to Know God

Now just a few thoughts on the way I can come to know God as the God above all circumstances, filling my heart and life every day. The one thing I need is this: I must wait upon God. The original translation of the verse is—it is in our Dutch version and it is in the margin too—"My soul is silent unto God." What is the silence of the soul unto God? A soul conscious of its littleness, its ignorance, its prejudices, and its dangers from passion, from all that is human and sinful. It is a soul conscious of that which says, "I want the everlasting God to come in and to take hold of me, and to take such hold of me that I may be kept in the hollow of His hand for my entire life. I want Him to take such possession of me that every moment He may work all in all in me." That is what is implied in the very nature of our God. How we ought to be silent unto Him and wait upon Him!

May I ask, with reverence, What is God for? God is for this: to be the light and the life of creation, the source and power of all existence. The beautiful trees, the green grass, and the bright sun were created so that they might show forth His beauty, His wisdom, and His glory. The tree that is one hundred years old—when it was planted, God did not give it a stock of life by which to carry on its existence. No, God clothes the lilies every year afresh with their beauty. Likewise, every year God clothes the tree with its foliage and its fruit. Every day and every hour it is God who maintains the life of all nature. And God created us so that we might be the empty vessels in which He could work out His beauty, His will, His love, and the likeness of His blessed Son. That is what God is for—to work in us by His mighty operation without one moment's ceasing.

When I begin to understand this, I no longer think of the true Christian life as a high impossibility and an unnatural thing. Then I can say, "It is the most natural thing in creation that God would have me every moment, and that my God would be nearer to me than all else." Just think, for a moment, what a mistake it is to imagine that I cannot expect God to be with me every minute. Just look at the sunshine; have you ever had any trouble as you were working or as you were studying or reading a book in the light the sun gives? Have you ever said, "Oh, how can I keep that light? How can I hold it fast and be sure that I will continue to have it to use?" You never thought that.

God has taken care that the sun will provide you with light. And, without your care, the light comes unbidden. I ask you: What do you think? Has God arranged that the light of that sun, which will one day be burned up, come to you unconsciously and abide in you blessedly and mightily? And is God not willing, or is He not able, to let His light and His presence so shine through you that you can walk all the day with God nearer to you than anything in nature? Praise God for the assurance: He can do it. And why does He not do it? Why so seldom and in such feeble measure? There is only one answer—you do not let Him. You are so occupied and filled with other things, spiritual things—preaching and praying, studying and working—so occupied with your faith, that you do not give God the time to make Himself known, to enter in, and to take possession, O brethren, listen to the word of the man who knew God so well, and begin to say, "My soul, wait thou only upon God."

I want to show that this is the very glory of the Creator, the very life Christ brought into the world, the life He lived, and the very life Christ wants to lift us up to, in its entire dependence on the Father. The very secret of the Christ-life is this—such a consciousness of God's presence that whether it was Judas, who came to betray Him, Caiaphas, who condemned Him unjustly, or Pilate, who gave Him up to be crucified, the presence of the Father was upon Him, within Him, and around Him so that man could not touch His spirit. And that is what God wants to be to you and to me. All your anxious restlessness and futile effort prove that you have not let God do His work. God is drawing you to Himself. This is not your own wish or the stirring of your own heart, but the everlasting, divine magnet that is drawing you. These restless yearnings and thirstings, remember, are the work of God. Come and be still and wait upon God. He will reveal Himself.

How to Wait on God

And how am I to wait on God? First of all, take more time in prayer, to be still before God without saying one word. And what is the most important thing in prayer? That I catch the ear of Him to whom I speak. We are not ready to offer our petition until we are fully conscious of having secured the attention of God. You tell me you know all that. Yes, you know it. But you need to have your heart filled by the Holy Spirit with the holy consciousness that the everlasting, almighty God is indeed very near you. The loving one is longing to have you for His own. Be still before God, wait, and say, "Oh, God, take possession. Reveal Yourself, not to my thoughts or imaginations, but by the solemn, awe-bringing, soul-subduing consciousness that God is shining upon me. Bring me to the place of dependence and humility."

Prayer may indeed be waiting on God, but there is a great deal of prayer that is not waiting on God. Waiting on God is the first and the best beginning for prayer. When we bow in the humble, silent acknowledgment of God's glory and nearness, there will be the very blessing, that we often get only at the end, even before we begin to pray. From the very beginning, I come face-to-face with God. I am in touch with the everlasting omnipotence of love, and I know my God will bless me. Let us never be afraid to be still before God. We will then carry that stillness into our work. When we go to church on Sunday or to the prayer meeting on weekdays, we will go with the desire that nothing may stand between us and God, and that we may never be so occupied with hearing and listening as to forget the presence of God.

Oh, that God might make every minister what Moses was at the foot of Mount Sinai; Moses led the people out to meet God, and they did meet Him until they were afraid. Let every minister ask, with all the earnestness his soul can command, that God may deliver him from the sin of preaching and teaching without making the people feel, first of all that, "He wants to bring us to God Himself." It can be felt, not only in the words, but in the very disposition of the humble, waiting, worshipping heart. We must carry this waiting into all our worship. We will have to make a study of it. We will have to speak about it. We will have to help each other, for the truth has been too much lost in the church of Christ. We must wait upon God for it. Then we will be able to carry it out into our daily life.

There are so many Christians who wonder why they fail. But think of the ease with which they talk and join in conversation, spending hours in it, never thinking that all this may be dissipating the soul's power and leading them to spend hours outside the immediate presence of God. I am afraid this is the great difficulty:

We are not willing to make the needed sacrifice for a life of continual waiting upon God. Are there not some of us who would feel it an impossibility to spend every moment under the covering of the Most High, *"in the secret of his tabernacle"* (Psalm 27:5)? Beloved, do not think it too high or too difficult. It is too difficult for you and me to attain, but our God will give it to us. Let us begin even now to wait more earnestly and intensely upon God. Let us, in our homes, bow in silence. Let us, in our closets, wait quietly and make a covenant. It may be that with our whole hearts, without words, we will seek God's presence to come in upon us.

What is Christianity? Just as much as you have of God working in you, that alone is Christianity. And if you want more faith, more grace, more strength, and more fruitfulness, you must have more of God. Let that be the cry of our hearts—More of God! More of God! More of God! And let us say to our souls, *"My soul, wait thou only upon God; for my expectation is from him"* (Psalm 62:5).

Chapter Four

Entrance into Rest

Chapter Four

Entrance into Rest

"Let us therefore fear, lest, a promise being left us of entering into his rest, any of you should seem to come short of it."
—Hebrews 4:1

"Let us labour therefore to enter into that rest, lest any man fall after the same example of unbelief."
—Hebrews 4:11

I want, in the simplest way possible, to answer the question: "How does a man enter into God's rest?" I also want to point out the simple steps that a man must take, all included in the act of surrender and faith.

There Is Rest

The first step, I think, is this: A man learns to say, "I believe, heartily, there is rest in a life of faith." Israel passed through two stages. This is beautifully expressed in the fifth chapter of Deuteronomy: "He brought us out, that He might bring us in"—two parts of God's work of redemption. "He brought us out from Egypt, that He might bring us into Canaan." (See Deuteronomy 5:6, 15). And that is applicable to every believer. At your conversion God brought you out of Egypt; and the same almighty God is longing to bring you into the Canaan life.

God brought the Israelites out, but they would not let Him bring them in. Because of this, they had to wander for forty years in the wilderness—the archetype, alas, of so many Christians. God brings them out in conversion, but they will not let Him bring them into all He has prepared for them. To a man who asks me, "How can I enter into the rest?", I say, first of all, speak this word: "I do believe that there is a rest into which Jesus, our Joshua, can bring a trusting soul." And if you want to know what the difference is between the two lives—the life you have been leading and the life you now want to lead—just look at the wilderness and Canaan.

What are the points of difference? In the wilderness there was wandering for forty years, backward and forward. In Canaan there was perfect rest in the land God gave them. That is the difference between the life of a Christian who has entered into Canaan and one who has not. The one who has not entered Canaan leads a life of wandering backward and forward, going after the world and coming back to repent. He is led astray by temptation and returns only to go off again—a life of ups and downs. In Canaan, on the other hand, there is a life of rest because the soul has learned to trust. "God keeps me every hour in His mighty power."

There is the second difference: The life in the wilderness was a life of want; in Canaan there was a life of plenty. In the wilderness there was nothing to eat, often not even water. God graciously supplied Israel's wants by the manna and the water from the rock. But, alas, the people were not content with this, and their lives were ones of want and murmurings. But in Canaan God gave them vineyards they had not planted, and the old corn of the land was there waiting for them. It was a land flowing with milk and honey, a land that lived by the rain of heaven and had the very care of God Himself. O Christian, come and say today, "I believe there is a possibility of such a change out of that life of spiritual death, darkness, sadness, and complaining, which I have often lived, and into the land of supply for every want." There the grace of Jesus is sufficient every day, every hour. Say today, "I believe in the possibility that there is such a land of rest for me."

And then, the third difference: In the wilderness there was no victory. When they tried to go up against their enemies, after sinning at Kadesh, they were defeated. In Canaan they conquered every enemy—from Jericho onward, they went from victory to victory. And so God waits, Christ waits, and the Holy Spirit waits to give victory every day. Not freedom from temptation, but, in union with Christ, a power that can say, *"I can do all things through Christ which strengtheneth me"* (Philippians 4:13). *"We are more than conquerors through him that loved us"* (Romans 8:37). May God help every heart to say that.

I Have Not Entered In

Then comes the second step. I want you to not only say, "I believe there is such a life," but also, "I have not yet had it." Say that. "I have never yet gotten that." Some may say, "I have sought it"; some may say, "I have never heard about it"; some may say, "At times I thought I had found it, but I lost it again." Let everyone be honest with God.

The Master's Indwelling

And now let all who have never yet found it honestly begin to say, "Lord, up to this time I have never had it." Why is it of such consequence to speak thus? Because, dear friends, some people want to glide into this life of rest gradually—to just quietly steal in. But God won't have it. Your life in the wilderness has not only been a life of sadness to yourself, but also a life of sin and dishonor to God. Every deeper entrance into salvation must always be by the way of conviction and confession.

Therefore, let every Christian be willing to say, "Alas, I have not lived that life, and I am guilty. I have dishonored God. I have been like Israel; I have provoked Him to wrath by my unbelief and disobedience. God have mercy on me!" Oh, let it go up before God—the secret confession: "I haven't done it. Alas, I have not glorified God by a life in the land of rest."

The Life of Rest

Then comes the third word I want you to speak and that is, "Thank God, that life is for me. " Some say, "I believe there is such a life, but not for me." There are people who continually say, "Oh, my character is so unstable. My will is naturally very weak. My temperament is nervous and excitable. It is impossible for me to always live without worry, resting in God."

Beloved, do not say that. You say so only for one reason: You do not know what your God will do for you. Do begin to look away from self and up to God. Take that precious word: *"I am the* L*ORD your God, which brought you forth out of the land of Egypt, to give you the land of Canaan"* (Leviticus 25:38). The God who took them through the Red Sea was the God who took them through Jordan into Canaan.

The God who converted you is the God who is able to give you, daily, this blessed life. Oh, begin to say, with the beginnings of a feeble faith, even before you claim it, if only intellectually, "It is for me. I do believe that. God does not disinherit any of His children. What He gives is for everyone. I believe that blessed life is waiting for me. It is meant for me. God is waiting to bestow it and to work it in me. Glory be to His blessed name! My soul says it is for me, too." Oh, take that little word *me,* and, looking up in the very face of God, dare to say, "This inestimable treasure—it is for me, the weakest and the unworthiest. It is for me." Have you said that? Say it now: "This life is possible for me, too."

Rest Comes from God

Then comes the fourth step: "I can never, by any effort of my own, grasp it. God must bestow it on me." I want you to be very bold in saying, "It is for me." But then I want you to fall down very low and say, "I cannot seize it. I cannot acquire it myself." And how can you then get it? Praise God, once He has brought you down into the consciousness of utter helplessness and self-despair, then He can draw nigh and ask you, "Will you trust your God to work this in you?" Dearly beloved Christian, say in your heart, "I never, by any effort, can take hold of God or seize this for myself. It is God who must give it." Cherish this blessed weakness. It is He who brought us out who Himself must bring us in. It is your greatest happiness to be weak.

Pray that God, by the Holy Spirit, will reveal to you this true weakness, which will open the way for your faith to say, "Lord, You must do it, or it will never be done." God will do it. People wonder, when they hear so many sermons about faith and such earnest pleadings to believe, why it is they cannot believe. There is just one answer: It is self. Self is working, is trying, is struggling, and it must fail. But when you come to the end of self and can only cry, "Lord, help me! Lord, help me!"—then the deliverance is near. Believe that. It was God who brought the Israelites in. It is God who will bring you in.

Give up Everything

One should be willing, for the sake of this rest, to give up everything. The grace of God is free. It is given without money and without price. And yet, on the other hand, Jesus said that every man who wants the pearl of great price must sacrifice his all, must sell all that he has to buy that pearl. It is not enough to see the beauty, the attractiveness, and the glory, to almost taste the gladness and the joy of this wonderful life as it has been set before you. You must become the possessor, the owner of the field. The man who found the field with a treasure and the man who found the great pearl were both glad. But they had not yet received it. They had found it, seen it, desired it, rejoiced in it, but they had not yet received it; not until they went and sold all, gave up everything, bought the ground, and bought the pearl.

Ah, friends, there is a great deal that has to be given up: the world, its pleasures, its favor, its good opinion. You are to stand in the same relationship to the world as Jesus did. The world rejected Him, cast Him out. You are to take up the position of your Lord, to whom you belong, and to follow with the rejected Christ. You have to give up everything. You have to give up all that is good in yourself and be humbled in the dust of death. And that is not all.

Your past spiritual life and experience and success—you have to give that all up and become nothing, so that God alone may have the glory. God has brought you out in conversion. It was God's own life that was given to you, but you have defiled it with disobedience and unbelief.

Give it all up. Give up all your own wisdom and your own thoughts about God's work. How hard it is for the minister of the Gospel to give up all his wisdom and to lay it at the feet of Jesus in order to become a fool, to be able to say, "Lord, I know nothing as I should know it. I have been preaching the Gospel, how little I have seen of the glory of the blessed land and the blessed life!"

Why is it that the blessed Spirit cannot teach us more effectively? No reason but this: The wisdom of man prevents it. The wisdom of man prevents the light of God from shining in. And we could say the same thing about other things. Give up all. Some may have an individual sin to give up. There may be a Christian man who is angry with his brother. There may be a Christian woman who has quarreled with her neighbor. There may be friends who are not living as they should. There may be a Christian holding a grudge about some little thing, not willing to surrender and leave the whole wilderness life and lust behind. Oh, do take this step and say, "I am ready to give up everything to have this pearl of great price. My time, my attention, my business—I count all subordinate to this rest of God as the first thing in my life. I yield all to walk in perfect fellowship with God." You cannot get that, and also live every day in perfect fellowship with God, without giving up time to it. You take time for everything.

How many hours a day has a young lady spent, for years and years, in order to become proficient on the piano? How many years does a young man study to prepare himself for the legal or medical profession? He gladly gives up hours and days and weeks and months and years to perfect himself for his profession. And do you think your faith is so cheap that, without giving time, you can find close fellowship with God? You cannot. But, my brothers and sisters, the pearl of great price is worth everything. God is worth everything. Christ is worth everything.

Oh, come today and say, "Lord, at any cost help me. I do want to live this life." And if you find it difficult to say this, if there is a struggle within your heart, never mind; say to God, "Lord, I thought I was willing, but I see how much unwillingness there is. Come and show me what evil still exists in my heart." By His grace, if you will lie at His feet and trust Him, you may depend on His divine deliverance.

Give Up Self to God

Then comes the fifth step, and that is to say—"I do now give myself up to the holy and everlasting God, for Him to lead me into this perfect rest." Ah, friends, we must learn to meet God face-to-face. My sin has been against God. David felt that when he said, *"Against thee, thee only, have I sinned"* (Psalm 51:4). It is God on the judgment seat whose face you will have to meet personally. It is God Himself who met you to pardon your sins. Come today and put yourself into the hands of the living God. God is love. God is near. God is waiting to give you His blessing. The heart of God is yearning for you. "My child," God says, "you think you are longing for rest. It is I that am longing for you, because I desire to rest in your heart as My home, as My temple." You need your God, yes, but your God needs you to find the full satisfaction of His Father-heart through Christ in you. Come today and say, "I do now give myself up to Christ. I have made the choice. I deliberately say, 'Lord God, I am the purchaser of the pearl of great price. I give up everything for it. In the name of Jesus, I accept that life of perfect rest.'"

Trust God for Rest

And then comes my last thought. When you have said that, then add—"And now, I trust God to make it all real to me in my experience. Whether I am to live one year or thirty years, I have heard today: 'God is Jehovah, the Great I Am of the everlasting future, the Eternal One. And thirty years hence is to Him just the same as now.' God gives Himself to me, not according to my power to hold Him but according to His almighty power of love to hold me."

Will you trust God today for the future? Oh, will you look up to God in Christ Jesus once again? A thousand times you have heard, thought, and thanked, "God has given us His Son." But will you not say today, "How could He not give me all things, every moment and every day of my life?" Say that in faith. "How could God not be willing to keep me in the light of His countenance, in the full experience of Christ's saving power? Did God make the sun to shine so brightly, and is the light willing to pour itself into every nook and corner where it can find entrance? And will not my God, who is love, be all the day willing to shine into this heart of mine, from morning to night, from year's end to year's end?" God is love and longs to give Himself to us.

O Christians, come; you have thus far lived a life in your own strength. Will you not begin today? Will you not choose a life in which God will be all, and in which you rest in Him for all? Will you not choose a life in which you will say, "O God, I ask, I expect, I trust You for it. I enter this day into the rest of God to let God keep me—to let God keep me every hour. I enter into the rest of God." Are you ready to say that? Be of good courage—fear not; you can trust God. He brings into rest. Listen to God's word to the prophets once again: *"Take heed, and be quiet; fear not, neither be fainthearted"* (Isaiah 7:4). Joshua brought Israel into the land. God did it through Joshua. And Jesus is your Joshua, your salvation. This is the Jesus who washed you in His blood, your Jesus, whom you have learned to know as a precious Savior. Trust Him today afresh: "O my Jesus, take me, bring me in, and I will trust You, and in You the Father." You may count on it; He will take you, and the work will be done.

Chapter Five

The Kingdom First

Chapter Five

The Kingdom First

"Seek ye first the kingdom of God."
—Matthew 6:33

You know what need there is for unity in Christian life and Christian work. And where is the bond of unity between the life of the church, the life of the individual believer, and the work to be done among non-Christians? One expression for that unity is: *"Seek ye first the kingdom of God."* That does not mean, as many people take it, "Seek salvation. Seek to get into the kingdom, then thank God, and rest there." Ah, no, the meaning of that word *"seek"* is entirely different and infinitely larger. It means letting the kingdom of God, in all its breadth and length, in all its heavenly glory and power, be the one thing you live for—and all other things will be added unto you.

The Kingdom First

"Seek ye first the kingdom of God." Let me try to answer two very simple questions: the one, "Why should the kingdom of God be first?"; and the other, "How can it be?" or "Why should it be so?" God has created us as reasonable beings. Because of this, the more clearly we see that something set before us is proper and an absolute necessity, according to the law of nature, we so much more willingly accept it and aim after it. And now why does Christ say this: *"Seek ye first the kingdom of God"*?

Look at God's Nature

If you want to understand the reason, look at God, and then look at man. Look at God. Who is God? The great Being for whom alone the universe exists, and in whom alone it can have its happiness. Creation came from Him; it cannot find any rest or joy but in Him.

Oh, that Christians understood and believed that God is a fountain of happiness—of perfect, everlasting blessedness! What would the result be? Every Christian would say, "The more I can have of God, the happier I will be. The more of God's will, the more of God's love, and the more of God's fellowship, the happier my life will be." If they believed that with their whole hearts, many Christians would, with the utmost ease, give up everything that separates them from God!

Why is it that we find it so hard to hold fellowship with God? A young minister once said to me, "Why is it that I have so much more interest in study than in prayer? Can you teach me the art of fellowship with God?" My answer was, "O my brother, if we have any true concept of what God is, the art of fellowship with Him will come naturally and will be a delight." Yes, if we believed God to be pure joy to the one who comes to Him, a fountain of unlimited blessing, how we would give up all for Him! Does joy not have a far stronger attraction than anything else in the world? Is it not the joy in every beauty, in every virtue, in every pursuit, that draws us toward it? And if we believe that God is a fountain of joy, sweetness, and power to bless, how our hearts will turn aside from everything and say, "Oh, the beauty of my God! I rejoice in Him alone." But, alas, to many the kingdom of God looks like a burden and something unnatural. It looks like a strain, and we seek some relaxation in the world. Then God is not our chief joy. I come to you with a message. It is right because of what God is as infinite love, as infinite blessing; and it is our highest privilege to listen to Christ's words. We must seek God and His kingdom first and above everything.

Why Was Man Created?

And then look at man again—man's nature. What was man created for? To live in the likeness of God and in His image. Now if we have been created in the image and likeness of God, we can find our happiness in nothing except what God finds His happiness in. The more like Him we are, the happier we will be. And in what does God find His happiness? In two things: everlasting righteousness and everlasting charity. God is righteousness everlasting. *"God is light, and in him is no darkness at all"* (1 John 1:5). The kingdom, the domination, the rule of God will bring us nothing but righteousness. *"Seek ye first the kingdom of God, and His righteousness"* (Matthew 6:33). If men only knew what sin really is, if they really longed to be free from everything like sin, what a grand message this would be!

Jesus comes to lead me to God and His righteousness. We were created to be like God, in His perfect righteousness and holiness. What a prospect! And in His love, too. The kingdom of God means this: There is, in God, a rule of universal love. He loves and loves and never ceases to love. And He longs to bless all who will yield to His pleadings. God is light, and God is love. And now the message comes to man. Can you think of a higher nobility? Can you think of anything more grand than to take the position that God takes and to be one with God in His kingdom—to have His kingdom fill your heart—to have God Himself as your King and portion?

My friends, let us remember that we must not just try to get a few of the blessings of the kingdom every now and then. But the glory of the kingdom is this: It is the kingdom of God where God is all in all. The French Empire, when Napoleon lived, had military glory as the ideal. Every Frenchman's heart thrilled at the name of Napoleon as the man who had given the empire its glory. If we realize what it means—our God takes us up into His kingdom; He puts His kingdom into us; and, with the kingdom, we have God Himself, that Blessed One, possessing us—surely there would be nothing that could move our hearts to enthusiasm like this.

The kingdom of God first! Blessed be His name! Look at man. I am not talking about man's sins, man's wretchedness, man's seeking everywhere for pleasure, rest, and deliverance from sin. But I am saying, Think about what man is by creation, and then think about what man is now by redemption. Let every heart say, "It is right. There is no blessedness or glory like that of the kingdom. The kingdom of God ought to be first in my whole life and being."

How to Make God's Kingdom First

But now comes the important question, "How can I attain this?" Here we come to the great question that is troubling the lives of tens of thousands of Christians throughout the world. And it is strange that it is so very difficult for them to find the answer. Imagine, tens of thousands of people are not able to give an answer, and others, when the answer is given, cannot understand it. The day the centurion found his joy in being devoted to the Roman Empire, it immediately took charge of him with all its power and glory. Dear friends, how are we to attain this blessed position in which the kingdom of God will fill our hearts with such enthusiasm so that it will spontaneously be first every day? The answer is: First of all, give up everything for it.

You have heard of the Roman soldier who gave up his soul, his affection, his life—who gave up everything—to be a soldier. And you have often seen in ancient and modern history how men who were not soldiers gave up their lives in sacrifice for a king or a country. Not many years ago, in the South African Republic, a war of liberty was fought. After three years of oppression by the English, the Africans said they would endure it no longer. So they gathered together to fight for their liberty. They knew how weak they were, compared to the power of the English, but they said, "We must have our liberty." They bound themselves together to fight for it, and when that vow had been made, they went to their homes to prepare for the struggle. Such a thrill of enthusiasm passed through that country that, in many cases, women, when their husbands might have been allowed to stay at home, said to them, "No, go, even though you have not been commanded." And there were mothers who, when one son was called out to the front, said, "No, take two or three." Every man and woman was ready to die. It was in very deed, "Our country first, before everything."

And even so, friends, it must be with you, if you want this wonderful kingdom of God to take possession of you. I pray by the mercies of God, give up everything for it. You might not know at once what that may mean, but take the words and speak them out at the footstool of God: "Anything, everything, for the kingdom of God." Persevere in that; and by the Holy Spirit, your God will begin to open to you the double blessing: on the one hand, the blessedness of the kingdom, which comes to possess your heart, and on the other hand, the blessedness of being surrendered to Him and sacrificing and giving up all for Him.

Keeping the Kingdom First

The kingdom of God first! How am I to reach that blessed life? The answer is, "Give up everything for it." And then a second answer would be this: "Live every day and hour of your life in the humble desire to maintain that position." There are people who hear this test, who say it is true, and assert that they want to obey it. But if you were to ask them how much time they spend with God day by day, you would be surprised and grieved to hear how little time they give up to Him. And yet they wonder why the blessedness of the divine life disappears. We prove the value we attach to things by the time we devote to them. The kingdom should be first, every day and all the day. Let the kingdom be first every morning. Begin the day with God, and God Himself will maintain His kingdom in your heart. Do believe that. Rome did its utmost to maintain the authority of the man who gave himself to live for it. And God, the living God, will He not maintain His authority in your soul if you submit to Him? He will, indeed. Come to Him—only come and give yourself up to Him in fellowship through Christ Jesus. Seek to maintain that fellowship with God all the day. Ah, friends, a man cannot have the kingdom of God first in his life and then occasionally, by way of relaxation, throw it off and seek his enjoyment in the things of this world. People secretly believe that life will become too solemn and too great a strain—it will be too difficult every moment of the day, from morning to evening—to have the kingdom of God first. One sees at once how wrong it is to think thus. The presence of the love of God must, every moment, be our highest joy. Let us say, "By the help of God, it will always be the kingdom of God first."

The Power of God's Spirit

And then, my last remark, in answer to that question, "How can it be?" is this: It can only be by the power of the Holy Spirit. Let us remember that God's Word comes to us with the language, *"Be filled with the Spirit"* (Ephesians 5:18). If you are content with less of the Spirit than God offers, not utterly and entirely yielding to be filled with the Spirit, you do not obey the command. But listen: God has made a wonderful provision. Jesus Christ came preaching the Gospel of the kingdom and proclaimed, *"The kingdom of heaven is at hand"* (Matthew 3:2).

"There be some standing here, which shall not taste of death, till they see the Son of man coming in his kingdom" (Matthew 16:28). He said to the disciples, *"Behold, the kingdom of God is within you"* (Luke 17:21).

And when did the kingdom come—that kingdom of God upon earth? When the Holy Spirit descended. On Ascension Day, the King went and sat down upon the throne at the right hand of God, and the kingdom of God, in Christ, the kingdom of heaven upon earth, was inaugurated. When the Holy Spirit came down, He brought God into the heart and established the rule of God in power. I am sometimes afraid that, in speaking of the Holy Spirit, we forget one thing. The Holy Spirit is often spoken of in connection with power, and it is right that we should seek power. However, the Holy Spirit is not as often spoken of in connection with the graces. And yet these are always more important than the gifts of power. Holiness, humility, meekness, gentleness, and lovingkindness are the true marks of the kingdom.

We speak rightly of the Holy Spirit as the only one who can breathe all this into us. But I think there is a third thing that is almost more important and often forgotten, and that is this: Through the Spirit, the Father and the Son themselves come.

The Master's Indwelling

When Christ first promised the Holy Spirit, and spoke about His approaching coming, He said,

> *At that day ye shall know that I am in my Father, and ye in me, and I in you. He that hath my commandments, and keepeth them, he it is that loveth me: and he that loveth me shall be loved of my Father, and I will love him, and will manifest myself to him....If a man love me, he will keep my words: and my Father will love him, and we will come unto him, and make our abode with him.*
>
> (John 14:20–21, 23)

Christian, if you want to have the kingdom of God first in your life, you must have the kingdom in your heart. If my heart is set on a thing, even if I am bound by chains, the moment the chains are loosened, I fly toward the object of my affection and desire. And likewise, the kingdom must be within us, and then it is easy to say, "The kingdom first." But to have the kingdom within us in truth, we must have God the Father and Christ the Son, by the Holy Spirit, within us, too. There is no kingdom without the King.

You are called to likeness with Christ. Oh, how many Christians strive after this part and that part of the likeness of Christ and forget the root of the whole? What is the root of all? That Christ gave Himself up entirely to God and His kingdom and glory. He gave His life that God's kingdom might be established. Do the same today. Give your life to God to be a continual living sacrifice, and the kingdom will come with power into your heart. Give yourself up to Christ. Let Christ the King reign in your heart, and the heavenly kingdom will come there. The presence and the rule of God will be known in power. Oh, think of that wonderful thing that is going to happen in the great eternity. We read of it in 1 Corinthians 15:28: God has entrusted Christ with the kingdom, but a day is coming when Christ Himself will come again to be subjected to the Father. He will give up the kingdom to the Father, so that God may be all, and in that day Christ will say before the universe, "This is My glory; I give back the kingdom to the Father!"

Christians, if your Christ finds His glory here on earth, in dying and sacrificing Himself for the kingdom and then in giving the kingdom to God in eternity again, will you and I not come to God to do the same? Will we not count anything we have as loss, that the kingdom of God may be made manifest and that God may be glorified?

Chapter Six

Christ Our Life

Chapter Six

Christ Our Life

"Christ, who is our life."
—Colossians 3:4

One question that rises in every mind is this: "How can I live that life of perfect trust in God?" Many do not know the correct answer or the full answer. It is this: "Christ must live it in me." That is why He became man. As a man, He lived a life of trust in God to show us how we ought to live. When He had completed His life on earth, He went to heaven so that He might do more than just show us. He went to heaven so that He might give us, and live in us, that life of trust. It is as we understand what the life of Christ is and how it becomes ours that we will be prepared to desire and to ask Him to live it in us Himself. Once we have seen what the life is, we will understand how He can actually take possession and make us like Himself.

I would especially like to direct your attention to that first question, "How can I live that life of perfect trust in God?" I wish to set before you the life of Christ as He lived it, so that you may understand what it is He has for us and what we can expect from Him. Christ Jesus lived a life on earth that He expects us to literally imitate. We often say that we long to be like Christ. We study the traits of His character, mark His footsteps, and pray for grace to be like Him. Yet somehow, we barely succeed. And why? Because we want to pluck the fruit while the root is absent. If we really want to understand what the imitation of Christ means, we must go to that which constituted the very root of His life before God. It was a life of absolute dependence, absolute trust, absolute surrender. And until we are one with Him in the principle of His life, it is futile to seek, here or there, to copy the graces of that life.

In the gospel story we find five great points of special importance: Christ's birth, His life on earth, His death, His resurrection, and His ascension. In these, we have what an old writer has called "the process of Jesus Christ." It is the process by which He became what He is today—our glorified King and our Life. In all this life process, we must be made like Him. Look at the first. What do we have to say about His birth? This: He received His life from God. What about His life upon earth? He lived that life in dependence upon God. About His death? He gave up His life to God. About His resurrection? He was raised from the dead by God. And about His ascension? He lives His life in glory with God.

Life from God

First, He received His life from God. And why is it so important for us to look to that? Because, in this act, Christ Jesus had the starting point of His whole life. He said, *"The living Father hath sent me"* (John 6:57); *"The Father loveth the Son, and hath given all things into his hand"* (John 3:35); *"The Father hath...given to the Son to have life in himself"* (John 5:26). Christ received it as His own life, just as God has His life in Himself. And yet all the time it was a life given and received. "Because the Father Almighty has given this life to Me, the Son of Man on earth, I can count on God to maintain it and to carry Me through all." And that is the first lesson we need. We need to meditate on it often. We need to pray, think, and wait before God until our hearts open to the wonderful consciousness that the everlasting God has a divine life within us that cannot exist except through Him.

I believe God has given us His life; its roots are in Him. I feel it must be maintained by Him. We often think that God has given us a life that is now our own, a spiritual life, and that we are to take charge. Then we complain that we cannot keep it right. No wonder; we must learn to live as Jesus did. I have a God-given treasure in this earthen vessel. I have the light of the knowledge of the glory of God. I have the life of God's Son within me, given to me by God Himself. And it can only be maintained by God Himself as I live in fellowship with Him.

What did the apostle Paul teach us in Romans 6? He had told us that we must reckon ourselves dead to sin and alive to God in Christ Jesus. He then went on to say, *"Yield yourselves unto God, as those that are alive from the dead"* (Romans 6:13). How often a Christian hears solemn words about his being alive to God and his having to reckon himself dead indeed to sin and alive to God in Christ! He does not know what to do. He immediately thinks, "How can I keep it, this death and this life?" Listen to what Paul said. The moment that you believe yourself dead to sin and alive to God, go with that life to God Himself. Present yourself as alive from the dead and say to God, "Lord, You have given me this life. You alone can keep it. I bring it to You. I cannot understand everything. I hardly know what I have, but I come to God to perfect what He has begun." To live like Christ, I must be conscious every moment that my life has come from God, and He alone can maintain it.

Dependence on God

How did Christ live out His life during the thirty-three years in which He walked here on earth? He lived it in dependence on God. You know how often He said, *"The Son can do nothing of himself"* (John 5:19), and *"The words that I speak unto you I speak not of myself: but the Father that dwelleth in me, he doeth the works"* (John 14:10). He waited unceasingly for the teaching, the commands, and the guidance of the Father. He prayed for power from the Father. Whatever He did, He did in the name of the Father. He, the Son of God, felt the need of much prayer, of persevering prayer, of bringing down from heaven and maintaining the life of fellowship with God in prayer. We hear a great deal about trusting God. And we may say, "Ah, that is what I want." And we may forget the secret of it all—that God, in Christ, must work all in us. I not only need God as an object of trust, but I must have Christ within me as the power to trust. He must live His own life of trust in me.

Look at it in the wonderful story of Paul, the apostle, the beloved servant of God. He was in danger of self-confidence, and God in heaven sent that terrible trial in Asia to bring him down lest he trust in himself and not in the living God. God watched over His servant that he would be kept trusting. Remember that other story about the thorn in the flesh, in 2 Corinthians 12; he was in danger of exalting himself, and the blessed Master came to humble him and to teach him: *"My grace is sufficient for thee: for my strength is made perfect in weakness"* (2 Corinthians 12:9).

If we are to enter into the rest of faith and to abide there—if we are to live the life of victory in the land of Canaan—it must begin here. We must be broken down from all self-confidence and learn to, like Christ, depend absolutely and unceasingly on God. There is a greater work to be done in that than perhaps we know. We must be broken down, and our souls must be in an unceasing attitude of, "I am nothing. God is all. I cannot walk before God as I should for one hour, unless God maintains the life He has given me." What a blessed solution God gives to all our questions and difficulties when He says,

The Master's Indwelling

"My child, Christ has gone through it all for you. Christ has worked out a new nature that can trust God. And Christ, the Living One in heaven, will live in you and enable you to live that life of trust." That is why Paul said, *"I have confidence in you through the Lord,"* (Galatians 5:10). What does this mean? Does it only mean through Christ as the mediator or intercessor? Surely not. It means much more: Through Christ living in and enabling us, we are able to trust God as Christ trusted Him.

Surrender to God

What does the death of Christ teach us of His relationship to the Father? It opens up to us one of the deepest and most solemn lessons of Christ-life, one that the church of Christ understands all too little. We know what the death of Christ means as an atonement, and we can never emphasize too much that blessed substitution and bloodshed, by which redemption was won for us. But let us remember, that is only half the meaning of His death. The other half is this: Just as much as Christ was my substitute, who died for me, He is also my head, in whom and with whom I die. And just as He lives for me, to intercede, He also lives in me, to carry out and to perfect His life. If I want to know about the life that He will live in me, I must look at His death. By His death, He proved that He possessed life only to hold it and to spend it for God. To the very uttermost, without the shadow of a moment's exception, He lived for God—every moment, everywhere, He held life only for His Father.

And so if one wants to live a life of perfect trust, he must perfectly surrender his life and his will, even unto death. He must be willing to go all lengths with Jesus, even to Calvary. When He was twelve years old, Jesus said, *"Wist ye not that I must be about my Father's business?"* (Luke 2:49). When He came to Jordan to be baptized, He said, *"It becometh us to fulfil all righteousness"* (Matthew 3:15). So on through all His life, He continually said, *"My meat is to do the will of him that sent me"* (John 4:34), and *"For I came down from heaven, not to do mine own will, but the will of him that sent me"* (John 6:38). *"Lo, I come to do thy will, O God"* (Hebrews 10:9). And in the agony of Gethsemane, Christ's words were, *"Not as I will, but as thou wilt"* (Matthew 26:39).

Someone says, "I do indeed desire to live the life of perfect trust. I want to let Christ live it in me. I am longing to have such an understanding of Christ that I will be certain that He will abide in me forever. I want to come to the full assurance that Christ, my Joshua, will keep me in the land of victory." What is necessary for that? My answer is, "Take care that you do not take a false Christ, an imaginary Christ, a half Christ."

And what is the full Christ? The full Christ is the man who said, "I give up everything to the death that God may be glorified. I have not a thought, I have not a wish, I would not live a moment, except for the glory of God." You at once say, "What Christian can ever attain that?" Do not ask that question, but ask, "Has Christ attained it, and does He promise to live in me?" Accept Him in His fullness and allow Him to teach you how far He can bring you and what He can work in you. Make no conditions or stipulations about failure, but cast yourself upon—abandon yourself to—Christ, who lived that life of utter surrender to God so that He might prepare a new nature that He could impart to you. A nature in which He might make you like Himself.

Then you will be on the path that leads you, with His help, on to blessed experience and possession of what He can do for you. Christ Jesus came into the world with a commandment from the Father that He should lay down His life. He lived with that one thought in His bosom His whole life long. And the one thought that ought to be in the heart of every believer is this: "I am dead with Christ. I am absolutely, unchangeably given up to wait on God, that God may work out His purpose and glory in me from moment to moment." Few attain the victory and the enjoyment and the full experience at once. But you can do this. Take the right attitude, and as you look to Jesus and what He was, say, "Father, You have made me a partaker of the divine nature, a partaker of Christ. It is in the life of Christ given up to You to the death, in His power and indwelling, in His likeness, that I desire to live out my life before You."

Death is a solemn thing, an awful thing. In the Garden, it cost Christ great agony to think of dying that death. No wonder it is not easy for us. But we willingly consent when we have learned the secret—in death alone the life of God will come. In death there is unspeakable blessedness. It was this that made Paul so willing to bear the sentence of death in himself; he knew the God who quickens the dead. The sentence of death is on everything that is of nature. But are we willing to accept it? Do we cherish it? Would we rather try to escape the sentence or forget it? We do not fully believe that the sentence of death is on us. Whatever is of nature must die. Ask God to make you willing to believe with your heart that to die with Christ is the only way to live in Him. You ask, "But must it then be dying every day?" Yes, beloved, Jesus lived every day in the prospect of the cross. We, in the power of His victorious life, being made conformable to His death, must rejoice every day in going down with Him into death.

Let me illustrate this point. Think of an oak tree that is a hundred years old. How was that oak born? In a grave. The acorn was planted in the ground, a grave was made for it that the acorn might die. It died and disappeared. Then it cast roots downward and shoots upward, and now that tree has been standing a hundred years. Where is it standing? In its grave. All the time, it has been in the very grave where the acorn died. It has stood there, stretching its roots deeper and deeper into that earth in which its grave was made. Yet all the time, though it stood in the very grave where it had died, it has been growing higher, stronger, broader, and more beautiful. And all the fruit it ever bore and all the foliage that adorned it year by year, it owed to that grave in which its roots are cast and kept.

Even so, Christ owes everything to His death and His grave. And we, too, owe everything to that grave of Jesus. Oh, let us live every day rooted in the death of Jesus. Do not be afraid, but say, "To my own will I will die. To human wisdom, human strength, and to the world, I will die. It is in the grave of my Lord that His life has its beginning, its strength, and its glory."

Raised by God

This brings us to our next thought. Christ received life from the Father; Christ lived His life in dependence on the Father; Christ gave His life up in death to the Father; and, finally, Christ received His life again raised by the Father, by the power of the glory of the Father. Oh, the deep meaning of the resurrection of Christ! What did Christ do when He died? He went down into the darkness and absolute helplessness of death. He gave up a life that was without sin—a life that was God-given, beautiful, and precious—and He said, "I will give it into the hands of My Father if He asks it." And He did it. He was there in the grave waiting on God to do His will. And because He honored God to the utmost in His helplessness, God lifted Him up to the very utmost of glory and power. Christ lost nothing by giving up His life in death to the Father. And so, if you want the glory and the life of God to come upon you, it is in the grave of utter helplessness that that life of glory will be born. Jesus was raised from the dead, and that resurrection power, by the grace of God, can and will work in us. Let no one expect to live a right life until he lives a full resurrection life in the power of Jesus. Let me state in a different way what this resurrection means.

Christ had a perfect life, given by God. The Father said: "Will You give up that life to Me? Will You part with it at My command?" And He parted with it; but God gave it back to Him in a second life infinitely more glorious than that earthly life. Likewise, God will give this glory-life to everyone who willingly consents to part with his life. Have you ever understood it? Jesus was born twice. The first time He was born in Bethlehem. That was a birth into a life of weakness. But the second time He was born from the grave. He is the *"firstborn from the dead"* (Colossians 1:18). Because He gave up the life that He had by His first birth, God gave Him the life of the second birth, in the glory of heaven and the throne of God.

Christian, that is exactly what we need to do. A man may be an earnest Christian. He may even be a successful worker or a Christian who has had a measure of growth and advancement. But if he has not entered this fullness of blessing, he needs to come to a second and deeper experience of God's saving power. He needs, just as God brought him out of Egypt through the Red

Sea, to come to a point where God brings him through Jordan into Canaan. Beloved, we have been baptized into the death of Christ. It is as we say, "I have had a very blessed life. I have had many blessed experiences, and God has done many things for me. But I am conscious that there is something wrong still. I am conscious that this life of rest and victory is not really mine."

Before Christ got His life of rest and victory on the throne, He had to die and give up all. Do it, too, and you will share His victory and glory with Him. It is as we follow Jesus in His death that His resurrection, power, and joy will be ours.

Exalted with God

The fifth and final step in His wondrous path was this: He was lifted up to be forever with the Father. Because He humbled Himself, God highly exalted Him. Where does the beauty and the blessedness of that exaltation of Jesus originate? For Himself, it began in His perfect fellowship with the Father. For others, it begins in participation in the power of God's omnipotence.

Yes, that was the fruit of His death. Scripture promises that, in the resurrection life, God will not only give us joy and peace that passes all understanding, victory over sin, and rest in God, but He will also baptize us with the Holy Spirit. Or, in other words, He will fill us with the Holy Spirit. Jesus was lifted to the throne of heaven that He might there receive from the Father the Spirit in His new, divine manifestation, to be poured out in His fullness. And as we come to the resurrection life—the life in the faith of Him who is one with us and sits upon the throne—we, too, may be partakers of the fellowship with Christ Jesus as He constantly dwells in God's presence. And the Holy Spirit will fill us, to work in us and out of us, in a way that we have never yet known.

Jesus got this divine life by depending absolutely on the Father during His life, depending on Him even in death. Jesus got that life in the full glory of the Spirit to be poured out by giving Himself up in obedience, surrendering to God alone, and allowing God, even in the grave, to work in His mighty power. And that very same Christ will live out His life in you and me. Oh, the mystery! Oh, the glory! And, oh, the divine certainty! Jesus Christ means to live out that life in you and me. Do you not think that we ought to humble ourselves before God? Have we been Christians so many years and realized so little what we are? I am a vessel set apart, cleansed, emptied, consecrated. I am just standing, waiting every moment for God, in Christ, by the Holy Spirit, to work out in me as much of the holiness and the life of His Son as pleases Him.

And until the church of Christ goes down into the grave of humiliation, confession, and shame, and until it comes to lay itself in the very dust before God—to wait upon God to do something new, something wonderful, something supernatural in lifting it up—it will remain feeble in all its efforts to overcome the world. Within the church, what lukewarmness, what worldliness, what disobedience, what sin! How can we ever fight this battle or meet these difficulties? The answer is: Christ, the Risen One, the Crowned One, the Almighty One, must come and live in the individual members. But we cannot expect this except as we die with Him.

I referred to the tree grown so high and beautiful, with its roots every day for a hundred years in the grave in which the acorn died. Children of God, we must go down deeper into the grave of Jesus. We must cultivate the sense of weakness, dependence, and nothingness until our souls walk before God every day in a deep and holy trembling. God keep us from being anything in our own power. God teach us to wait on Him that He may work in us all He worked in His Son, until Christ Jesus may live out His life in us! For this, may God help us!

Chapter Seven

Christ's Humility, Our Salvation

Chapter Seven

Christ's Humility, Our Salvation

"Let this mind be in you, which was also in Christ Jesus...he humbled himself, and became obedient unto death, even the death of the cross."
—Philippians 2:5, 8

All Christians are familiar with this wonderful passage. Paul was speaking about one of the most simple, practical things in daily life—humility. In connection with that, he gave us a wonderful exhibition of divine truth. In this chapter, we have the eternal Godhead of Jesus—He was in the form of God and one with God (verse 6). We have His incarnation—He came down and was found in the likeness of man (Philippians 2:8). We have His death with the atonement—He *"became obedient unto death"* (verse 8). We have His exaltation—*"God also hath highly exalted Him"* (verse 9). We have the glory of His kingdom—that every knee shall bow, and every tongue confess Him (verse 10–11).

How did the apostle present this? As a theological study? No. Did he give a description of what Christ is? No. He prsented it as a simple, downright call to a life of humility in our fellowship with each other. Our life on earth is linked to all the eternal glory of the Godhead as revealed in the exaltation of Jesus. The very looking to Jesus, the very bowing of the knee to Jesus, ought to be inseparably connected with a spirit of the very deepest humility. Consider the humility of Jesus. First of all, that humility is our salvation. Then, that humility is just the salvation we need. And again, that humility is the salvation that the Holy Spirit will give us.

The Humility of Christ

Humility is the salvation that Christ brings. That is our first thought. We often have very vague—I might also say visionary—ideas of what Christ is. We love the person of Christ; but that which makes up Christ, which actually constitutes Him as the Christ, we do not know or love. If we love Christ above everything, we must love humility above everything, for humility is the very essence of His life and glory and the salvation He brings. Just think of it. Where did it begin? Is there humility in heaven? You know there is, for they cast their crowns before the throne of God and the Lamb. But is there humility on the throne of God? Yes; what was it but heavenly humility that made Jesus on the throne willing to say, "I will go down to be a servant, and to die for man. I will go and live as the meek and lowly Lamb of God"?

Jesus brought humility from heaven to us. It was humility that brought Him to earth, or He would never have come. In accordance with this, just as Christ became a man in this divine humility, so His whole life was marked by it. He might have chosen another form in which to appear. He might have come in the form of a king, but He chose the form of a servant. He made Himself of no reputation; He emptied Himself; He chose the form of a servant. He said, *"The Son of man came not to be ministered unto, but to minister, and to give his life a ransom for many"* (Matthew 20:28). And you know, in the last night He took the place of a slave, girded Himself with a towel, and went to wash the feet of Peter and the other disciples.

Christ's Humility, Our Salvation

Beloved, the life of Jesus upon earth was a life of the deepest humility. It was this that gave His life its worth and beauty in God's sight. And then, His death—possibly you haven't thought of it much in this connection—was an exhibition of unparalleled humility. *"He humbled himself, and became obedient unto death, even the death of the cross."* My Lord Jesus Christ occupied a low place during His time on earth. He took a very low place when He began to wash the disciples' feet. But when He went to Calvary, He took the lowest place there was to be found in the universe of God, the very lowest. He let sin, the curse of sin, and the wrath of God cover Him. He took the place of a guilty sinner that He might bear our load; that He might serve us in saving us from our wretchedness; that He might, by His precious blood, win deliverance for us; that He might, by that blood, wash us from our stain and our guilt.

We often think about Christ as God, as man, as the Atonement, as the Savior, and as exalted upon the throne, and we form an image of Christ. However, the real Christ, that which is at the very heart of His character, remains unknown. What is the real Christ? Divine humility, bowed down into the very depths for our salvation. The humility of Jesus is our salvation. We read, *"He humbled himself....Wherefore God also hath highly exalted him"* (Philippians

2:8–9). The secret of His exaltation to the throne is this: He humbled Himself before God and man. Humility is the Christ of God, and now, in heaven, that Christ, the Man of humility, is on the throne of God. What do I see? A Lamb standing, as if it had been slain, on the throne (Revelation 5:6); in glory, He is still the meek and gentle Lamb of God. His humility is the badge He wears there.

You often use that name—the Lamb of God—and you use it in connection with the blood of the sacrifice. You sing the praise of the Lamb, and you put your trust in the blood of the Lamb. Praise God for the blood. You can never trust that too much. But I am afraid you forget that the word *Lamb* must mean two things to us: It must mean not only a sacrifice, the shedding of blood, but it must also mean the meekness of God, incarnate upon earth, the meekness of God represented in the meekness and gentleness of a little Lamb.

Man Needs Humility

But the salvation that Christ brought is not only a salvation that flows out of humility—it also leads to humility. We must understand that this is not only the salvation that Christ brought, but that it is exactly the salvation that you and I need. What is the cause of all the wretchedness of man? Primarily, it is pride—man seeking his own will and his own glory. Yes, pride is the root of every sin, and so the Lamb of God comes to us in our pride and brings us salvation from it. We need, above everything, to be saved from our pride and our self-will. It is good to be saved from the sins of stealing, murdering, and every other evil, but a man needs to be saved from the root of all sin—his self-will and his pride.

It is not until man begins to feel this is exactly the salvation he needs that he can really understand what Christ is and accept Him as his salvation. This is the salvation that we as Christians and believers especially need. We know the sad story of Peter and John—what their self-will and pride brought upon them. They needed to be saved from nothing except themselves, and that is the lesson we must learn if we are to enter the life of rest. And how can we enter that life and dwell there in the bosom of the Lamb of God if pride rules? Have we not often heard complaints of how much pride exists in the church of Christ? What causes all of the division, strife, and envying that is often found even among God's saints? Why is it that in a family there is often bitterness—it may be only for half an hour or half a day, but what causes hard judgments and hasty words? What causes estrangement between friends? What causes evil-speaking? What causes selfishness and indifference to the feelings of others? Simply this: the pride of man. He lifts himself up, and he claims the right to have his opinions and judgments as he pleases. The salvation we need is indeed humility, because it is only through humility that we can be restored to our right relationship with God.

"Waiting on God"—that is the only true expression for the real relationship of the believer to God: to be nothing before God. What is the essential idea of a being made by God? It is this: to be a vessel in which He can pour out His fullness, in which He can exhibit His life, His goodness, His power, and His love. A vessel must be empty if it is to be filled. If we are to be filled with the life of God, we must be utterly empty of self. This is the glory of God, that He is to fill all things and, more especially, His redeemed people. And as this is the glory of man, so this is the only redemption and the only glory of every redeemed soul—to be empty and as nothing before God, to wait upon Him and to let God be all in all.

Humility has a prominent place in almost every epistle of the New Testament. Paul said,

Christ's Humility, Our Salvation

"With all lowliness and meekness, with longsuffering, forbearing one another in love; endeavouring to keep the unity of the Spirit in the bond of peace" (Ephesians 4:2–3).

The nearer you get to God and the more fully you know Him, the lowlier you will become. And you will love to be humble before God and man. We know of Peter's early self-confidence; but in his epistles he spoke a different language. He wrote there: *"Ye younger, submit yourselves unto the elder. Yea, all of you be subject one to another....Humble yourselves therefore under the mighty hand of God, that he may exalt you in due time"* (1 Peter 5:5–6). He understood, and he dared to preach, humility to all. It is indeed the salvation we need.

What is it that prevents people from coming to that entire surrender that we speak of? It is simply that they do not dare abandon themselves and trust themselves to God. They are not willing to be nothing, to give up their wishes, their will, and their honor to Christ. Will we refuse the salvation that Jesus offers? He gave up His own will. He gave up His own honor. He gave up any confidence in Himself. He lived dependent upon God as a servant whom the Father had sent. This is the salvation we need—the Spirit of humility that was in Christ.

The Master's Indwelling

What is it that often disturbs our hearts and our peace? It is pride seeking to be something. And God's decree is irreversible, *"God resisteth the proud, but giveth grace unto the humble"* (James 4:6). How often Jesus had to speak to His disciples about it! You will find repeatedly in the Gospel those simple words: *"Whosoever exalteth himself shall be abased; and he that humbleth himself shall be exalted"* (Luke 14:11). He taught His disciples: *"Whosoever will be chief among you, let him be your servant"* (Matthew 20:27). This should be our one cry before God: "Let the power of the Holy Spirit come upon me, with the humility of Jesus, that I may take the place that He took." Beloved, do you want a better place than Jesus had? Are you seeking a higher place than Jesus? Or will you say, "Down, down, as deep as I can ever go. With the help of God, I will be nothing before God. I will be where Jesus was."

Humility: The Key to the Spirit

And now comes the third thought—This is the salvation the Holy Spirit brings. You know what a change took place in those disciples. Let us praise God for it. The Holy Spirit means this: the life, the disposition, the temper, and the inclination of Jesus, brought down from heaven into our hearts. That is the Holy Spirit. He has His mighty workings to bestow as gifts.

But the fullness of the Holy Spirit is this: Jesus Christ, in His humility, coming to dwell in us. When Christ was teaching His disciples, all His instructions may have helped in the way of preparation, breaking them down, making them conscious of what was wrong, and awakening their desire. But the instruction could not do it, and all their love to Jesus and their desire to please Him could not do it, until the Holy Spirit came.

That is the promise Christ gave. He said, in connection with the coming of the Holy Spirit, *"I will come again"* (John 14:3). Christ said to His disciples, in essence, "I have been three years with you, you have been in the closest contact with Me, and I have done the utmost to reach your hearts. I have sought to get into your hearts, yet I have failed. But, fear not, I will come again. In that day, you will see Me, your hearts will rejoice, and no man will take your joy from you. I will come again to dwell in you and live My life in you." Christ went to heaven so He might get a power that He never had before. And what power was that? The power of living in men. God be praised for this! It was because Jesus—the humble One, the Lamb of God, the meek, the lowly, and the gentle One—came down in the Holy Spirit into the hearts of His disciples, so that the pride was expelled, and the very breath of heaven breathed through Him in the love that made them one heart and one soul.

Dear friends, Christ is yours. Christ, as He comes in the power of the Holy Spirit, is yours. Are you longing to have Him, to have the perfect Christ Jesus? Come, then, and see how, amid the glories of His Godhead, His atonement, and His exaltation—which is the chief and brightest glory—He humbled Himself from heaven down to earth and on earth down to the cross. He humbled Himself to bear the name, show the meekness, and die the death of the Lamb of God. And what is it we now need to do? How are we to be saved by this humility of Jesus? It is a solemn question; but, thank God, the answer can be given.

How to Possess Humility

First, we must desire it above everything. Let us learn to pray for God to deliver us from every vestige of pride, for this is a cursed thing. Let us learn to set aside other things in the Christian life and begin to plead with the Lamb of God day by day, "O Lamb of God, I know Your love, but I know so little of Your meekness." Come day after day and lay your heart against His heart. Say to Him with strong desire, "Jesus, Lamb of God, give me Yourself, with Your meekness and humility," and He will fulfill the desires of those who fear Him. It is not enough to desire it and to pray for it; claim and accept it as yours. This humility is given to you in Christ Jesus. Christ is our life. What does that mean? Oh, that God might give you and me a vision of what that means! The air is our life, and the air is everywhere, universal. We breathe without difficulty because God surrounds us with the air. And is the air nearer to me than Christ is? The sun gives light to every green leaf and every blade of grass, shining hour by hour and moment by moment. And is the sun nearer to the blade of grass than Christ is to man's soul? Surely not. Christ is around us on every side. Christ is pressing on us to enter, and there is nothing in heaven, earth, or hell that can keep the light of Christ from shining into the heart that is empty and open.

If the windows of your room were closed with shutters, the light could not enter. It would be on the outside of the building, streaming and streaming against the shutters, but it could not enter. But leave the windows without shutters, and the light rejoices to come in and fill the room. Even so, children of God, Jesus and His light, Jesus and His humility, are around you on every side, longing to enter into your hearts. Come and take Him today in His blessed meekness and gentleness. Do not be afraid of Him; He is the Lamb of God. He is so patient with you, so kind toward you, and so tender and loving.

Take courage today and trust Jesus to come into your heart and take possession of it. And when He has taken possession, there will be a life of blessed, daily fellowship with Him. You will feel a necessity for ever deeper quiet time with Him, for worshipping and adoring Him, and for just sinking down before Him in helplessness and humility and saying, "Jesus, I am nothing, and You are all." It will be a blessed life because you will be conscious of being at the feet of Jesus. At this moment, you can claim Jesus in His divine humility as the life of your soul. Will you? Will you not open your heart and say, "Come in; come in"?

Come today; take Him up afresh in this blessed power of His wonderful humility, and say to Him, "O my Lord, You who said, *'Learn of me; for I am meek and lowly in heart'* (Matthew 11:29), I know why I do not have the perfect life. It is because of my pride; but today, come and dwell in my heart. You, who led even Peter and John into the blessedness of Your heavenly humility, You will not refuse me. Lord, here I am. Do, by Your wonderful humility, which alone can save, come in. O Lamb of God, I believe in You; take possession of my heart and dwell in me."

When you have said that, go out in quiet and retire, walking gently as if you are holding the Lamb of God in your heart. Say, "I have received the Lamb of God. He makes My heart His care. He breathes His humility and dependence on God into me and so brings me to God. His humility is my life and salvation."

Chapter Eight

The Complete Surrender

Chapter Eight

The Complete Surrender

"And Joseph was brought down to Egypt; and Potiphar, an officer of Pharaoh, captain of the guard, an Egyptian, bought him of the hands of the Ishmeelites, which had brought him down thither. And the LORD was with Joseph, and he was a prosperous man; and he was in the house of his master the Egyptian. And his master saw that the LORD was with him, and that the LORD made all that he did to prosper in his hand."
—Genesis 39:1–3

We have, in this passage, an object lesson that teaches us what Christ is to us. Note: Joseph was a slave, but God was with him so distinctly that his master could see it.

> *And his master saw that the* L*ORD was with him, and that the* L*ORD made all that he did to prosper in his hand. And Joseph found grace in his sight, and he served him: and he made him overseer over his house.* (Genesis 39:3–4)

That was something new. Joseph had been a slave, but he became a master.

> *And he made him overseer over his house, and all that he had he put into his hand. And it came to pass from the time that he had made him overseer in his house, and over all that he had, that the* L*ORD blessed the Egyptian's house for Joseph's sake; and the blessing of the* L*ORD was upon all that he had in the house, and in the field. And he left all that he had in Joseph's hand; and he knew not ought he had, save the bread which he did eat. And Joseph was a goodly person, and well favoured.* (Genesis 39:4–6)

We find that Joseph had two roles in the house of Potiphar; first as a servant and a slave, one who was trusted and loved, but still entirely a servant; second, as a master. Potiphar made him overseer of his house, his lands, and all that he had. Then we read that he left everything in Joseph's hands, and he knew of nothing except the bread that came to his table. I want to call your attention to Joseph as a type of Christ. We sometimes speak, in the Christian life, of entire surrender, and it is right to do so. Here we have a beautiful illustration of what it is.

First, Joseph was in Potiphar's house to serve him and to help him. Joseph did that, and Potiphar learned to trust him so that he said, "All that I have I will give into his hands." Now that is exactly what should happen with a great many Christians. They know Christ, they trust Him, they love Him, but He is not Master; He is just a sort of a helper. When there is trouble, they come to Him. When they sin, they ask Him for pardon in His precious blood. When they are in darkness, they cry to Him. They more often live according to their own will, though, and seek help from themselves. But how blessed is the man who comes and, like Potiphar, says, "I will give up everything to Jesus!"

There are many who have accepted Christ as their Lord but have never yet come to the final, absolute surrender of everything. Christians, if you want perfect rest, abiding joy and strength to work for God, come and learn from that poor heathen Egyptian what you ought to do. He saw that God was with Joseph, and he said, "I will give up my house to him." Oh, learn to do that. There are some who have never yet accepted Christ, some who are seeking after Him, thirsting and hungering, but they do not know how to find Him.

Let me direct your attention to four thoughts regarding this surrender to Christ: First, its *motives;* second, its *measures;* third, its *blessedness*; and last, its *duration.*

Motives of Surrender to Christ

Its motives. What moved Potiphar to do this? I think the answer is very easy: He was a trusted servant of the king. He had the king's work to take care of, and he very likely did not have enough time to take care of his own house. All his time and attention were required at the court of Pharaoh. He had his duty there; he was in high honor, but his own house was neglected. Very likely he had had other overseers, one slave appointed to rule the others, and perhaps that one had been unfaithful or dishonest. In any case, his house was not as he would have liked it to have been. So he bought another slave, just as he had formerly done; but this time he saw something he had never seen before. There was something unusual about the man. He walked so humbly. He served so faithfully, so lovingly, and was so successful in everything. Potiphar began to look into the reason for this and finally concluded that God was with him.

It is a grand thing to have a man, blessed of God, to entrust one's business to. The heathen realized this; and because of the need in his own house and because of what he saw in Joseph, he decided to make Joseph overseer. These two motives most urgently plead that you say, "I will make Jesus master over my whole being." Your house, Christian, your spiritual life, the dwelling, the temple by God in your heart—what state is your heart in? Is your heart more often like the temple of old, in Jerusalem, that had been defiled and made a house of merchandise and afterward a den of thieves? Is your heart, meant to be the home of Jesus, often full of sin and darkness, full of sadness, full of vexation? You have done your very best to get it changed. You have called in the help of man and the help of means. You have used every method you can think of for getting it put right. But it will not come right until He, whose it is, comes in to take charge.

If there is any trouble in your heart, if you are in darkness or under the power of sin, I bring to you the Son of God with the promise that He will come in and take charge. As Potiphar took Joseph, will you not take Jesus? Has He not proven Himself worthy to be trusted? Come and say, "Jesus will have entire charge. He is worthy." Do not think only of His divine power, but think also of His wonderful love. Think of His coming from heaven to save you. Think of His dying on Calvary and shedding His blood out of intense love for you. Oh, think of it, Christ in heaven loves everyone who is given to Him, and whom He has made a child of God. *"Having loved his own which were in the world, he loved them unto the end"* (John 13:1).

Must I plead in the name of the love of the crucified Jesus? Must I plead with you Christians saying, "Look at Jesus, the Son of God, your Redeemer," and ask you to make Him overseer over all? Give Him charge of your temper, your heart's affections, your thoughts, your whole being, and He will prove Himself worthy of it. Joseph had been, for a time, just a common slave, and had served Pharaoh with the other slaves. Many a Christian has used Christ for his own advancement and comfort, just as he uses everything in the world. He uses father and mother, minister, money, and everything else the world will give, to comfort and make him happy. Likewise, there is danger of his using Christ Jesus in the same way. But Christian, this is not right. You are His house, and He has a right to dwell therein. Will you not come and surrender all and say, "Lord Jesus, I have made You overseer over all"?

The Measure of Surrender

The measure of that surrender. We read in the fourth verse of Genesis 39: *"All that he had he put into his hand."* Then in verse 5: *"And it came to pass from the time that he made him overseer over all that he had"*—there you have it the second time. *"The Lord blessed the Egyptian's house, and the blessing of the Lord was upon all that he had"*—there the third time. Then in verse 6: *"And he left all that he had"*—there you have the words the fourth time—*"in Joseph's hand; and he knew not ought he had, save the bread which he did eat."* What do I see here? I see that Potiphar actually put everything into Joseph's hands. He made him master over his slaves. Even all of his money was put into Joseph's hands, for we read that Potiphar had care of nothing. When dinner was brought upon the table, he ate of it; and that was all he knew of what was going on in his house. Is this not entire surrender? He put everything into the hands of Joseph.

Ah, beloved Christians, I want you to ask yourselves: "Have I done that?" You have offered more than one consecration prayer, and you have more than once said, "Jesus, all I have I give to You." You have said it and meant it. But, very probably, you did not fully realize what it meant.

There always seems to be a larger and more comprehensive meaning to the word *surrender.* We do not succeed in carrying out our intentions, because we take back one thing and another until we have lost sight of our original intention. Beloved Christians, let Christ Jesus have all. Let Him have your whole heart with its affections; He Himself loves with more love than Jonathan. (See 1 Samuel 18:1.) Let Him have your whole heart, saying, "Jesus, every fiber of my being, every power of my soul, will be devoted to You." He will accept that surrender. He spoke a solemn word: *"He that loveth father or mother more than me is not worthy of me"* (Matthew 10:37). Say today, "Lord Jesus, the love to father and mother, to wife and children, to brother and sister, I give up to You. Teach me how to love You. I have only one desire, which is to love You. I want to give my whole heart to be full of Your love."

But when you have given your heart, there is still more to give. There is the head—the brain with its thoughts. I believe Christians do not know how much they rob Christ by reading so much of the literature of the world. They are often so occupied with their newspapers that the Bible holds a very small place. O friends, I beg you, bring this noble power that God has given you—the power of a mind that can think heavenly, eternal, and infinite things—and lay it at the feet of

Jesus. Say, "Lord Jesus, every faculty of my being I want to surrender to You so You can teach me what to think and how to think for You and Your kingdom."

Bless God, there are men who have given their intellect to Jesus, and it has been accepted by Him. And, in this connection, there is my whole outer life. There is my relationship to society, my position among men, and my fellowship in my own home, with friends and family. My money, my time, my business, all these should be put in the hands of Jesus. One cannot know ahead of time the blessedness of this surrender, but blessed it surely is. Come, because He is worthy. Come, because you know you cannot keep things right yourself. Make Christ master over all you have. Give father, mother, wife, child, house, land, and money all to Jesus, and you will find that, in giving all, you receive it back one hundredfold.

The Blessings of Surrender

Look at the blessing of the entire surrender. Here you have the remarkable words:

> *And it came to pass from the time that he had made him overseer in his house, and over all that he had, that the* LORD *blessed the Egyptian's house*

for Joseph's sake; and the blessing of the LORD was upon all that he had in the house, and in the field.
(Genesis 39:5)

I ask you, Christians, if God did this to that unbelieving man, because he honored Joseph, if God, for Joseph's sake, blessed that Egyptian in this wonderful way, a Christian may surely venture to say, "If I put my life into the hands of Jesus, I am sure God will bless all that I have." Oh, dare to say it. Potiphar trusted Joseph implicitly and absolutely, and there was prosperity everywhere because God was with Joseph. Beloved friends, if you would only surrender everything, depend upon it, the blessing from that time would be yours. There would be a blessing within your own inner life and a blessing to your outer life. He blessed Potiphar in the house, in the field, everywhere.

O Christian, what is the blessing that you will get? I cannot tell all, but I can tell you this: If you will come to Christ Jesus and surrender all, the blessing of God will be on all that you have. There will be a blessing for your own soul. *"Thou wilt keep him in perfect peace, whose mind is stayed on thee"* (Isaiah 26:3). Try that. Trust Jesus for everything, trust everything to Him, and the blessing of God will come upon you—the sweet rest, the rest of faith. It is all in the hands of Jesus. He will guide you; He will teach you; He will work in you; He will keep you. He will be everything to you. What a blessed rest and freedom from responsibility and from care, because it is all in the hands of Jesus! I do not say trouble and trial will never come. But in the midst of trial and trouble, you will have the all-sufficiency of the presence of Jesus to be your comfort, your help, and your guide.

Joseph was sold by his brothers, but he saw God in it and was quite content. Christ was betrayed by Judas, condemned by Caiaphas, and given over to execution by Pilate; but in all that, Christ saw God and was content. Give over your life, in all its phases, into the hands of Jesus. Do this, remembering that the very hairs of your head are numbered, and not a sparrow falls to the earth without the Father's notice. Consent now and say, "I will give up everything into the hands of Jesus. Whatever happens is His will regarding me. Whether He comes in the light or in the dark, in the storm or on the troubled sea, I will rest in that blessed assurance. I give up my whole life entirely to Him."

In reading the book of Jonah, we find God's hand in each step of Jonah's experience. It was God who sent the storm when Jonah went aboard the ship, who appointed a whale to swallow him, and who ordered the whale to cast him out. Then afterward, it was God who caused the hot wind to blow when the sun was sending down its scorching rays, until the soul of Jonah was grieved. It was God who made the gourd grow, who sent the worm to kill the gourd, and who sent a sea-wind to dry the gourd up quickly. Thus we can see that every circumstance of our living, every comfort and every trial, comes from God in Christ. There is nothing that can touch a hair of my head. Not a sharp word comes against me; an unexpected flurry will not surround me, because it is all Jesus. With my life in His hands, I do not need to care for anything. I can be content with what Jesus gives.

God blessed Potiphar in the field and in the visible life outside of his house. And God will bless you, so that, in your fellowship with men, you may be a blessing. By your holy, humble, respectful, quiet walk, you may carry comfort. By your loving readiness to be a servant and a helper to all, you may show what the Spirit of God has done within you. O my brother, my sister, you have no concept of it—neither have I—how God is willing to bless the soul that is utterly given up to Jesus. God can delight in nothing but Jesus. God delights infinitely in Jesus. God longs to see nothing in us but Jesus. If I give up my heart and life to Jesus and say, "My God, I want you to see nothing in me but Jesus," then I bring to the Father the sacrifice that is the most acceptable of all. O believers, come today—come out of all your troubles and all your self-efforts and your self-confidence—and let the blessed Son of God take possession.

Surrender Lasts Forever

Let me direct your thoughts, lastly, to the duration of this surrender. I want to emphasize this, because in many cases the surrender does not last. Some go away, and for a time have much gladness and joy. But soon it begins to decrease, and in a few weeks or perhaps months, the joy is all gone. Others who do not lose their surrender entirely complain sadly that, at times, it goes away and comes again. They say, "My life has been very much blessed since that surrender I made to God, but it has not always been on the same level." What did Potiphar do? We read in the fourth verse: *"He made him overseer over his house...and he left all that he had in Joseph's hand."* What a simple word! He *left* it there.

And, children of God, if you will only get to that point and say, "For all eternity, I leave it in the hands of Jesus," you will find what a blessing it is. Potiphar found now that he could do the king's business with two hands and an undivided heart. I might try to rescue a drowning man by holding on to something firmly with one hand while I reach out with the other hand to the man. But it is a wonderful thing for a person to be able to stretch out both hands, and that person is the one who has left all with Jesus—all his inner life, all his cares and troubles—and has entirely given himself up to do the will of God. Will you leave it there? I must emphasize this, because I know that temptations will come.

One temptation will be that the feelings you had in your act of surrender will pass away; they will not be as strong. Another temptation will be that circumstances will tempt you. Beloved, temptations will come; God means them for your good. Every temptation brings you a blessing. Do understand that. Learn the lesson of giving up everything to Jesus, and let Jesus take charge of everything. Leave all with Jesus. Do not think that by a surrender today or on any other day, however powerful, however mighty, things will remain all right by themselves. Every morning, when God wakes you, you need to put your heart, your life, your house, and your business into the hands of Jesus. Wait on Him if need be, in silence or in prayer, until He gives you the assurance, "My child, for today all is safe. I take charge."

And morning by morning, He will renew the blessing. Morning by morning, you will go out from your quiet time in the consciousness that, "Today I have had fellowship with my King, and it is all right. Jesus has taken charge." And so, day by day, you can have grace to leave all in the hands of Jesus.

In conclusion let me speak to two classes. There are times when your heart is restless; there are also times when you are afraid to die. There are some true believers who have perhaps never yet understood that it was their duty to give up everything to Christ. Beloved fellow Christians, I come with a message from your Father: Come today and take that word into your hearts and upon your lips, even though you do not understand it. "Jesus, I make You Master of everything, and I will wait at Your feet, that You can show me what You want me to be and do." Do it now. And let me say to believers who have done it before and who long with an unutterable longing to do it fully and perfectly—children of God, you can do it, for the Holy Spirit has been sent down from heaven for this one purpose: to glorify Jesus. He will glorify Jesus in your heart by letting you see how perfectly Jesus can take possession of the whole heart. He will glorify Jesus by bringing Him into your very life, that your whole life may shine out with the glory of Jesus.

Depend upon it, the Father will give it to you by the Holy Spirit, if you are ready. Oh, come, and let your communion with God be summed up in a simple prayer and answer—"My God, as much as You will have of me to fill with Christ, You may have today." "My child, as much of Christ as your heart longs to have, you will have; for it is My delight that My Son be in the hearts of My children."

Chapter Nine

Dead with Christ

Chapter Nine

Dead with Christ

"I am crucified with Christ."
—Galatians 2:20

The Revised Version more precisely states the above text as, *"I **have been** crucified with Christ"* (emphasis added). In this connection, let us read the story of a man who was literally crucified with Christ. We may use the entire narrative of Christ's work upon earth in the flesh as a type of His spiritual work. Let us take, in this instance, the story of the penitent thief, Luke 23:39–43. I think we may learn from him how to live as men who are crucified with Christ.

Paul said, *"I have been crucified with Christ."* And, again: *"God forbid that I should glory, save in the cross of our Lord Jesus Christ, by whom the world is crucified unto me, and I unto the world"* (Galatians 6:14). We often ask earnestly: How can I be free from the self-life? The answer is, Get another life. We often speak about the power of the Holy Spirit coming upon us, but I doubt if we fully realize that the Holy Spirit is a heavenly life, come to expel the selfish, fleshly, and earthly life. If we want, in very deed, to fully enjoy the rest that there is in Jesus, we can only have it as He comes in—in the power of His death—to slay what is in us of nature, to take possession, and to live His own life in the fullness of the Holy Spirit.

God's Word takes us to the cross of Christ and teaches us two things about that cross. It tells us that Christ died for sin. We understand what that means—that in His atonement He died as I never die, as I can never die, as I need never die. He died for sin and for me. But what gave His death such power to atone? It was this: the spirit in which He died; not the physical suffering, not the external act of death, but the spirit in which He died. And what was that spirit? He died to sin. Sin had tempted Him, surrounded Him, and had brought Him very close to saying, "I cannot die." In Gethsemane, He cried, *"Father...take away this cup from me"* (Mark 14:36). But God be praised, He gave up His life rather than yield to sin. He died to sin, and, in dying, He conquered. And now, I cannot die for sin like Christ, but I can and I must die to sin like Christ. Christ died for me. In that, He stands alone. Christ died to sin, and in that I have fellowship with Him. I have been crucified; I am dead.

We Are Dead with Christ

And here is the great subject to which I want to lead you—What is it to be dead with Christ? And how is it that I can practically enter into this death with Christ? We know that the greatest characteristic of Christ is His death. From eternity He came with the commandment of the Father that He should lay down His life on earth. He gave Himself up to it, and He set His face toward Jerusalem. He chose death. And He lived and walked on earth to prepare Himself for death. His death is the power of redemption. Death gave Him His victory over sin, His resurrection, His new life, His exaltation, and His everlasting glory. The great mark of Christ is His death.

Even in heaven, upon the throne, He stands as the Lamb that was slain. Through eternity, they sing, *"Thou art worthy...for thou wast slain"* (Revelation 5:9). Beloved brethren, your Boaz, your Christ, your all-sufficient Savior, is a

Man of whom the chief mark and the greatest glory is this: He died. And if the bride is to live with her husband as His wife, then she must enter into His state, into His spirit, and into His nature. She must forever be as He is. If we are to experience the full power of what Christ can do for us, we must learn to die with Christ.

I should not, perhaps, use that expression, "We must learn to die with Christ." I should say, rather, "We must learn that we are dead with Christ." That is a glorious thought in the sixth chapter of Romans. To every believer in the church of Rome—not to the select ones or the advanced ones, but to every believer in the church of Rome, however feeble—Paul wrote, *"We be dead with Christ"* (Romans 6:8). On the strength of that, he said, *"Reckon ye also yourselves to be dead indeed unto sin"* (Romans 6:11). What does that mean, "You are dead to sin"? We cannot see it more clearly than by referring to Adam. Christ was the second Adam. What happened in the first Adam? I died in the first Adam. I died to God; I died in sin. When I was born I had the life of Adam in me, which had all the characteristics of the life of Adam after he had fallen. Adam died to God—Adam died in sin—and I inherit the life of Adam. Thus I am dead in sin as he was, and dead to God.

But at the very moment I begin to believe in Jesus, I become united to Christ, the second Adam. And as truly as I am united by my birth to the first Adam, I am made partaker of the life of Christ. What life? The life that died to sin on Calvary and that rose again. Therefore, God, by His apostle, tells us, *"Reckon ye also yourselves to be dead indeed unto sin, but alive unto God through Jesus Christ our Lord"* (Romans 6:11). You are to believe it to be true, because God says it—for your new nature is indeed, in virtue of your vital union to Christ, actually and utterly dead to sin.

If we want to have the real Christ, whom God has given us—the real Christ who died for us—in the power of His death and resurrection, we must take our stand here. But many Christians do not understand what the sixth chapter of the epistle to the Romans teaches us. They do not know that they are dead to sin. They do not know it, and, therefore, Paul instructed them, *"Know ye not, that so many of us as were baptized into Jesus Christ were baptized into his death?"* (Romans 6:3). How can we, who are dead to sin in Christ, live any longer therein? We indeed have the death and the life of Christ working within us. But, alas, most Christians do not know this and, therefore, do not experience or practice it. They need to be taught that their first need is to be brought to the recognition, to the knowledge, of what has taken place in Christ on Calvary and what has taken place in their becoming united to Christ.

The man must begin to say, even before he understands it, "In Christ, I am dead to sin." It is a command: *"Reckon ye also yourselves to be dead indeed unto sin"* (Romans 6:11). Get hold of your union to Christ. Believe in the new nature within you—the spiritual life that you have from Christ, a life that has died and been raised again. A man's acts are always in accordance with his idea of his state. A king acts like a king. Otherwise, if he acts out of character, we say, "That man has forgotten his kingship." But if a man is conscious of being a king, he behaves like a king. And so I cannot live the life of a true believer unless I am fully conscious of being dead to sin in Christ. I must say, "I thank God that I am dead in Christ. Christ died unto sin, and I am united with Christ. Christ lives in me and I am dead to sin."

Christ's Life in Me

What life does Christ live in me? Ask, instead, what life does Adam live in me? Adam lives in me the death life, a life that has fallen under the power of sin and death—death to God. Adam lives that life in me by nature as an unconverted man. And Christ, the second Adam, has come to me with a new life. I now live in His life, the death-life of Christ. As long as I am unaware of it, I cannot act according to it, though it is in me. Praise God, when a man begins to see what it is and then begins in obedience to say, "I will do what God's Word says. I am dead; I believe myself dead," then he enters into a new life. On the strength of God's everlasting Word, your union to Christ, and the great fact of Calvary, believe; know yourself as dead to sin. A man must see this truth; this is the first step.

The second is, he must accept it in faith. And then what? When he accepts it in faith, then he struggles. It is a painful experience, for that faith is still very feeble. He begins to ask, "But why, if I am dead to sin, do I commit so much sin?" And the answer God's Word gives is simply this: You do not allow the power of that death to be applied by the Holy Spirit. We need to understand that the Holy Spirit came from heaven, from the glorified Jesus, to bring His death and His life into us. The two are inseparably connected. Christ died to sin, and He lives to God. The death and the life in Him are inseparable. Likewise, in us, the life to God in Christ is inseparably connected with the death to sin.

And that is what the Holy Spirit will teach us and work in us. If I have accepted Christ in faith by the Holy Spirit and have yielded myself to Him, He will not leave me. He will reveal the full power of my fellowship in His death and life in my heart. To some this undoubtedly comes in a single moment of supreme power and blessing. All at once they see and accept it and enter in. Death to sin is a divine experience. The tendency to evil is not rooted out. No, but the power of Christ's death can keep us from sin and destroy the power of sin. The power of Christ's death is manifested in the Holy Spirit's unceasingly mortifying the deeds of the body. Someone asks me if growth is still necessary. Undoubtedly. By the Holy Spirit, a man can now begin to live and grow, deeper and deeper, in the fellowship of Christ's death. A man may be filled with the Holy Spirit, and yet have great imperfections. Why? Perhaps his heart has not been fully prepared by a complete discovery of sin. There may be pride, self-consciousness, impatience, or other qualities that he has never noticed. The Holy Spirit does not always cast these out at once.

No, there are different ways of entering into the blessed life. One man enters into the blessed life with the idea of power for service. Another may enter with the idea of rest from worry and weariness. Another may enter with the idea of deliverance from sin. In all these aspects, something is limited. Therefore, every believer is to give himself up after he knows the power of Christ's death, and say continually, "Lord Jesus, let the power of Your death work through me, penetrating my whole being." As the man gives of himself unreservedly, he will begin to bear the marks of a crucified man. The apostle said, "I have been crucified," and he lived like a crucified man.

Marks of a Crucified Man

What are the marks of a crucified man? The first is deep, absolute humility. Christ humbled Himself and became obedient unto death, even the death of the cross. When death to sin begins to work mightily, that is one of its chief and most blessed proofs. It breaks a man down, and the great longing of his heart is, "Oh, that I could be more humble before my God and be nothing at all, that the life of Christ might be exalted. I deserve nothing but the cursed cross. I give myself over to it." Humility is one of the great marks of a crucified man.

Another mark is helplessness. When a man hangs on the cross, he is utterly helpless and can do nothing. As long as we Christians are strong and can work or struggle, we do not enter into the blessed life of Christ. But when a man says, "I am a crucified man. I am utterly helpless, every breath of life and strength must come from my Jesus," then we learn what it is to sink into our own inability and say, "I am nothing."

Still another mark of crucifixion is restfulness. Yes; Christ was crucified, went down into the grave, and we are crucified and buried with Him. There is no place of rest like the grave. A man can do nothing there. *"My flesh also shall rest in hope"* (Psalm 16:9), said David and said the Messiah. And yes; when a man goes down into the grave of Jesus, it means that he cries out, "I have nothing but God, I trust God. I am waiting upon God; my flesh rests in Him. I have given up everything, that I may rest, waiting upon what God is to do in me."

Remember, the crucifixion, the death, and the burial are inseparably one. Recall that the grave is the place where the mighty resurrection power of God will be manifested. And remember those precious words in the eleventh chapter of John: *"Said I not unto thee, that, if thou wouldest believe, thou shouldest see the glory of God?"* (John 11:40). Christ spoke those words at the grave of Lazarus. Where will I see the glory of God most brightly? Beside the grave. Go down into death believing, and the glory of God will come upon you and fill your heart.

Dear friends, we want to die. If we are to live in the rest and the peace and the blessedness of our great Boaz—if we are to live a life of joy and of fruitfulness, of strength and of victory—we must go down into the grave with Christ. The language of our life must be: "I am a crucified man. God be praised, though I have nothing but sin in myself, I have an everlasting Jesus, with His death and His life, to be the life of my soul." How can I enter into this fellowship of the cross? We find an illustration of this in the story of the penitent thief. Thomas said, before Christ's death, *"Let us also go, that we may die with him"* (John 11:16). And Peter said, *"Lord, I am ready to go with thee, both into prison, and to death"* (Luke 22:33). But the disciples had all failed. Our Lord took a man who was the filth of the earth, and He hung him upon the cross of Calvary beside Himself, saying to Peter and to all: "I will let you see what it is to die with Me." And He says that word today to the weakest and the humblest. If you are longing to know what it is to enter into death with Jesus, come and look at the penitent thief.

A Penitent Heart

And what do we see there? First of all, we see the state of a heart prepared to die with Christ. We see, in that penitent thief, a humble, wholehearted confession of sin. There he hung upon the cursed tree, and the multitudes were blaspheming that man beside him. But he was not ashamed to publicly confess, "I am dying a death that I have deserved. I am suffering justly. This cross is what I deserve." Here is one of the reasons why the church of Christ enters so little into the death of Christ. Men do not want to believe that the curse of God is upon everything in them that has not died with Christ.

People talk about the curse of sin, but they do not understand that the whole nature has been infected by sin and that the curse is on everything. Has my intellect been defiled by sin? Terribly, and the curse of sin is on it. Therefore, my intellect must go down into the death. Ah, I believe that the church of Christ suffers more today from trusting in intellect, in fleshly wisdom, in culture, and in mental refinement, than from almost anything else. The spirit of the world comes in, and men seek, by their wisdom and their knowledge, to help the Gospel. Yet they rob it of its crucifixion mark. Christ directed Paul to go and preach the Gospel of the cross but not to do it with words of wisdom. The curse of sin is on all nature. If there is a minister who has delighted in preaching, who has done his very best, who has given his very best in the way of talent and of thought, and who asks, "Must that go down into the grave?", I say, "Yes, my brother, the whole man must be crucified."

It is likewise with the heart's affection. What is more beautiful than the love of a child to his mother? In that lovely nature, there is something unsanctified. It must be given up to die. God will raise it from the dead and give it back again, sanctified and made alive unto God. People often say to me, "But God has made all things so beautiful. Is it not right that we enjoy them? Are His gifts not all good?" I answer, "Yes, but remember what it says: They are good, if sanctified by the Word of God and prayer." The curse of sin is on them. The blight of sin is on everything, even the most beautiful. It takes God's Word and prayer to sanctify them. It is very hard to give up a thing to the death. It is hardest of all to give up my life to the death. And I never will until I have learned that everything about my life is stamped by sin. I must let it go down into the death as the only way to have it quickened and sanctified.

The penitent thief confessed his sin and that he deserved death. Then he had faith in the almighty power of Christ. A wonderful faith. It has no parallel in the Bible. There hung the cursed malefactor with Jesus of Nazareth. He dared to speak and say, *"For we receive the due reward of our deeds....And he said unto Jesus, Lord, remember me when thou comest into thy kingdom"* (Luke 23:41–42). Oh, that we might learn to believe in the almighty power of Christ! That man believed that Christ was a King and had a kingdom. He believed that He would take him up in His arms, in His heart, and remember him when He came into His kingdom. He believed that, and believing it, he died.

Brethren, you and I need to take time to come to a much larger and deeper faith in the power of Christ. We must believe that the almighty Christ will indeed take us in His arms and carry us through this death-life, revealing the power of His death in us. I cannot live without personal contact with Christ every hour of the day. Christ must do it; Christ can do it. Come, therefore, and say, "He is the almighty One. He came from the throne of God to prove his omnipotence. And the Father proved it when He rose from the dead." Would you be afraid, now that Christ is on the throne, of doing what the malefactor did when Christ was on the cross. Would you entrust yourself to Him to live as one dead with Him? Christ will carry you through the very process He went through. He will make His death work in you every day of your life.

I note one thing more in the penitent thief—his prayer. There was his conviction of sin, but even better, the utterance of his faith in prayer. He turned to Jesus. Remember that the whole world, with perhaps the exception of Mary and the women, had turned against Christ that day. Of the whole world of men, as far as I know, there was only that one praying to Christ. Do not wait to see what others do. If you wait for that—I say it in love and tenderness—you will not find much company in the church of Christ. Pray incessantly, "Lord Christ, let the power of Your death come into me." For God's sake, pray the prayer. If you want to live the life of heaven, there must be death to sin in the power of Jesus. There must be personal entrustment of the soul into His death to sin, personal acceptance of Jesus to do the mighty work.

Fellowship with Christ

We have seen how the man prepared for death. Let us look, second, at how Christ met him. He met him, you know, with that wonderful promise, with its three wonderful parts:

"Today shalt thou be with me in paradise" (Luke 23:43). In that one phrase, there is a promise of fellowship with Christ; a promise of rest in eternity, in the Paradise from which sin had cast man out; and a promise of immediate blessing. With that three-fold blessing, Jesus comes to you and me and says, "Believer, are you longing to live the Paradise life, where I give souls to eat of the Tree of Life, in the Paradise of God, day by day? Are you longing for that uninterrupted communion with God that there was in Paradise before Adam fell? Are you longing for perfect fellowship with Me, longing to live where I am living, in the love of the Father? Today, today, even as the Holy Spirit says, 'Today you will be with Me!' Do you long for Me? I long more for you. Do you long for fellowship? I long unceasingly for your fellowship, for I need your love, My child, to satisfy My heart. Nothing can prevent My receiving you into fellowship. I have taken possession of heaven for you, as the Great High Priest, that you might live the heavenly life, that you might have access into the holiest of all and an abiding dwelling place there. Today, if you so desire, you will be with Me in Paradise."

Thank God, the Jesus of the penitent thief is my Jesus. Thank God, the cross of the penitent thief is my cross. I must confess my sinfulness if I want to come into the closest communion with my blessed Lord. There was not a man on earth during the thirty-three years of Christ's life that had such wonderful fellowship with the Son of God as the penitent thief. For, with the Son of God, he entered the glory. What made him so different from the others? He was on the cross with Jesus and entered Paradise with Him. And if I live on the cross with Jesus, the Paradise life will be mine every day.

And now, if Jesus gives me that promise, what have I to do? Let go. When a ship is moored alongside the dock, with everything ready for the start, the last bell is rung, and the order given, "Let go." Then the last rope is loosened, and the steamer moves. There are things that tie us to the earth, to the flesh-life and to the self-life. But listen to the message that comes to us today: "If you want to die with Jesus, let go." You need not understand all. It may not be perfectly clear; the heart may appear dull, but never mind. Jesus carried that penitent thief through death to life. The thief did not know where he was going; he did not know what was to happen. But Jesus, the mighty conqueror, took him in His arms and landed him, in his ignorance, in Paradise.

Oh, I have sometimes said in my soul, bless God for the ignorance of that penitent thief. He knew nothing about what was going to happen, but he trusted Christ. And if I cannot understand all about this crucifixion with Christ, the death to sin, the life to God, and the glory that comes into the heart, never mind; I trust my Lord's promise. I cast myself helpless into His arms. I maintain my position on the cross. Given up to Jesus, to die with Him, I can trust Him to carry me through.

Each one of us must take the blessed opportunity of doing what Ruth did when she, in obedience to the advice of her mother, just cast herself at the feet of the great Boaz, the redeemer, to be his. Will we not come into personal contact with Jesus, and just speak, before the world, these simple words: "Lord, here is this life. There is still much of self, sinfulness, and self-will in it, but I come to You. I long to fully enter into Your death. I long to fully know that I have been crucified with You. I long to live Your life every day." Then say, "Lord Jesus, I have seen Your glory, what You did for the penitent one at Your side on the cross. I am trusting You, that You will do it for me. Lord, I cast myself into Your arms."

Chapter Ten

Joy in the Holy Spirit

Chapter Ten

Joy in the Holy Spirit

"For the kingdom of God is not meat and drink; but righteousness, and peace, and joy in the Holy Ghost."
—Romans 14:17

In this text we have the earthly revelation of the work of the Trinity. The kingdom of God is righteousness, which represents the work of the Father. The foundations of His throne are justice and judgment. Then comes the work of the Son: He is our peace, our Shiloh, our rest. The kingdom of God is peace; not only the peace of pardon for the past, but also the peace of perfect assurance for the future. Not only is the work of atonement finished, but the work of sanctification is also finished in Christ. And I may receive and enjoy what is prepared for me. The new man has been created, and I may, in Him, live out my life. If a kingdom is established in righteousness, if the rule is perfect, there can be perfect rest. If there is peace, no war from without and no civil dissension within, a nation can be happy and prosperous.

And so, after righteousness and peace comes the joy, the blessed happiness in which a man can live: *"The kingdom of God…is righteousness, and peace, and joy in the Holy Ghost."* May we regard this joy of the Holy Spirit, not only as a beautiful thing to admire, not only as a thing to have beautiful thoughts about, but also as a blessing that we are going to claim.

We often see a fruit market or bakery with beautiful fruit or cakes temptingly displayed in the window. There is a great pane of plate glass before it, and the hungry little boys stand there and look and long, but they cannot reach it. If you were to say to one, "Now, little boy, take that fruit," he would look at you in surprise. He has learned that there is something between himself and the fruit. If he had never known about glass, he might attempt it. The plate glass is sometimes so clear that even a grown man might for a moment be deceived and stretch out his hand. But he soon finds there is something invisible between him and the fruit. This exactly represents the life of many Christians;

they see, but they cannot take. And what is this invisible pane of plate glass that hinders my taking the beautiful things I see? It is nothing but the self-life. I see divine things but cannot reach them; the self-life is the invisible plate glass.

We are willing, working, and striving, yet we are holding something back. We are afraid to give up everything to God. We do not know what the consequences may be. We have not yet comprehended that God and Christ Jesus are worth everything. Whatever is told to us about the blessed life of peace and joy, we say, "Praise God. God's Word is true. I believe the Word." And yet, day by day, we stand back. When someone says, "Take it," we say, "I can't take it. There is something between." If only we were willing to give up the self-life and had the courage to give it up today and let the joy of the Holy Spirit be our assurance. That is the faith God has prepared for us. That is the faith we can claim—not only righteousness, not only peace, but the joy of the Holy Spirit. That is the kingdom of God.

Christ in Your Heart

What is this joy? First of all, it is the joy of the presence of Jesus. We are often inclined to speak more of two other things, the power for sanctification and the power for service. But I find the fact that the Holy Spirit came from heaven to be the abiding presence of Christ in His disciples, in the church, and in the heart of every believer to be more important than either of those two things, the power for sanctification or the power for service. The Lord Jesus was going away, and His disciples were very sad. Their hearts were sorrowful. But He said to them, *"I will see you again, and your heart shall rejoice, and your joy no man taketh from you"* (John 16:22). What took place with them may take place with us, too. The Holy Spirit is given to make the presence of Jesus an abiding reality, a continual experience.

And what was that joy that no man could ever touch? It was the joy of Pentecost. And what was Pentecost? The coming of the Lord Jesus in the Holy Spirit to dwell with His disciples. While Jesus was with His disciples on earth, He could not get into their hearts in the right way. They loved Him, but they could not take in His teaching, could not partake of His disposition, could not receive His very Spirit into their being. But when He had ascended to heaven, He came back in the Spirit to dwell in their hearts. It is this alone that will help us to go on: the minister to his congregation with its difficulties; the businessman to his counter; the mother to her large family with its care; the worker to her Bible class. It is only this that will help us to feel, "I can conquer; I can live in the rest of God." Why? "Because I have the almighty Jesus with me every day."

A Hindrance to Faith

With God's people, there seems to be one hindrance: They do not know their Savior. They do not realize that this blessed Christ is an ever-present, all-pervading, indwelling Christ who wants to take charge of their entire lives. They do not know or believe that He is an almighty Christ and ready, in the midst of any difficulties and any circumstances, to be their keeper and their God. This is absolutely true. Many Christians are asked how one may have the joy unspeakable, the joy that nothing can take away, the joy of the friendship and nearness and love of Jesus filling his heart. We complain that the rush of competition is so terrible that we cannot find time for private prayer. Beloved, the Lord Jesus Christ, if He comes to you as a brother and a friend and an abiding guest, can give your heart the joy of the Holy Spirit, so that business will take its right place under your feet. Your heart is too holy to have it filled with business. Let the business be in the head and under the feet. But let Christ have the whole heart, and He will keep the whole life.

Our glorious, exalted, almighty, ever-present Christ! Why is it that you and I cannot trust Him fully and perfectly to do His work? We must say, before God, that we do trust Him, that we will trust Christ to be, every moment, all that we can desire. On the cross of Calvary, Christ was all alone, and you believe He did a perfect and a blessed work. Christ in heaven is all alone, as High Priest and Intercessor, and you trust Him for His work there. But, praise God, it is equally true that Christ in the heart is able, all alone, to keep the heart continually. May it please God to reveal to His children the nearness of Christ standing and knocking at the door of every heart, ready to come in and rest forever there, to lead the soul into His rest.

The Joy of the Lord

We all know what the power of joy is. We know there is nothing as attractive as joy, there is nothing that can help a man to bear and endure as much as joy. We know that the Lord Jesus Himself endured the cross for the joy that was set before Him. One is not living correctly if he is living a sighing, trembling, doubting life. Come today and believe the joy of the Holy Spirit is meant for you. Does the Scripture not say, *"Whom having not seen, ye love; in whom, though now ye see him not, yet believing, ye rejoice with joy unspeakable and full of glory"* (1 Peter 1:8)? Do you not believe that this blessed, adorable, inconceivably beautiful Son of God, the delight of the Father, could fill your heart with delight day and night if He were always present? And do you not believe that He loves you more than a bridegroom loves his bride? Do you not believe that, having bought you with His blood, Jesus is longing for you? He needs you to satisfy His heart of love. Begin to believe with your whole heart, "The joy of the Holy Spirit is my portion," for the Holy Spirit secures, without interruption, the presence and the love of Jesus.

The Deliverance of the Spirit

Second, there is the joy of deliverance from sin. The Holy Spirit comes to sanctify us. Christ is our sanctification, and the Holy Spirit comes to communicate Him to us—to work out all that is in Christ and to reproduce it in us. Let us remember that, in the sight of God, there is something more than work. There is Christlikeness—the likeness and the life of Christ in us.

This is what God wants; this will prepare us for work. God does not ask that the Christ-life be separate from our life like a temple full of filthy, impure, foul creatures with Christ hidden away somewhere there. That is not the intention of God. He wants Christ so formed in us that we are one with Christ, and that in our thinking, feeling, and living, the image of His blessed Son is manifest before Him. The Holy Spirit is given to sanctify us.

My friends, are you willing to be sanctified from every sin, be that sin great or small? I am not asking, "Do you feel that you have the power to conquer it?" I am not even asking, "Do you feel the power to cast it out?" It may be that you feel no power—that will not hinder if you are willing. I cannot cast out sin, but I can ask the almighty Christ by the Holy Spirit to do it. I can say to Christ, "There is the sin; there is the evil thing. I lay it at Your feet, and cast it there. I cast it into Your very bosom. Lord, I am ready to cut off the right hand, anything; only deliver me from it." Then Christ will cast out the evil spirit and give deliverance. The Spirit of God is a holy spirit, and His work is to free us from the power of sin and death.

And if you want to live in the joy of the Holy Spirit, you must ask yourself, "Am I willing to surrender everything that is sinful, even that which appears good, unto the Lord?" You may be involved in relationships that make your life very difficult. A pastor may be brought into very difficult relationships with his people. Or a businessman, with his partner or with those whom he has to associate, may be in an exceedingly trying position. But is not the blessed Lamb of God worth it all? What is the Christ worth to you? The question was once asked of the disciples, *"What think ye of Christ?"* (Matthew 22:42). I ask, "What is Christ worth to you?" And I plead with you, whatever prospective difficulties there may be and whatever perplexities surround you, take the whole world today and cast it at His feet. To have Him is worth any difficulty. To have Him will be the solution of every difficulty.

There are not only external, manifest difficulties and perplexities, there are also a thousand little things that come into our lives and often disturb us. There are temptations to unloving feelings, sharp words, and hasty judgments. Oh, come and believe that the Holy Spirit, the Sanctifier, can come in, rule, and give grace to pass through all hardship without sinning. Then you will know what the joy of the Holy Spirit is. Our body, we read in first Corinthians, is the temple of the Holy Spirit. It is to be holy in things like eating and drinking. How often a Christian realizes that he takes or seeks too much enjoyment in eating—eating for pleasure—and has no self-denial or self-sacrifice in his feeding the body! How often we tempt one another to eat, and how often the believer forgets that his body is the very secret temple of the Holy Spirit. Therefore, every mouthful we eat and drink must be for the glory of God in such a way as to be perfectly well-pleasing to Him.

The Way to Rest

Beloved, I bring you a message: There is access for you into the rest of God, and the Holy Spirit is given to bring you in. The Holy Spirit will fill your heart with the unutterable joy of Christ's presence. You will also know the joy of deliverance from sin, of victory over sin, the unutterable joy of knowing that you are doing God's will and are pleasing in His sight—knowing that He is sanctifying and keeping the temple for Christ to dwell in. Believers, the joy of the Holy Spirit, the joy of that holiness of God, is His blessedness, His purity, His perfection, which nothing can mar or stain or disturb. The Holy Spirit waits to bring and to manifest it in our lives. He wants to come so into our hearts that we will live as Holy Spirit people, with the sanctifying power of Jesus running through our whole beings.

The Unity and Rest of Love

My third thought is: The joy of the Holy Spirit is the joy of the love of the saints. The Holy Spirit was not given to any man on the day of Pentecost separate from the others. He came and filled the whole company. We know how much division, separation, and pride there had been among them; but on that day, the Holy Spirit so filled their hearts that it was said, "Behold how these men love one another." There was a love in the early church that the very heathen noticed and could not understand. Why was that? The Holy Spirit is the bond of union between the Father and Son, and that bond is love. The Holy Spirit is the love of God come to dwell in the heart. When He dwells with me and my brother, we learn to love each other. Although I am unloving by nature, and though I have very little grace, if the heart of my brother is full of the Holy Spirit, he loves me in spite of it all.

You know, love is a wonderful thing. As long as a person tries to love, it is not real love. But when real love comes, the more opposition it meets, the more it triumphs; for the more it can exercise itself and perfect itself, the more it rejoices. Take a mother with a son who dishonors her. How her love follows him! When she sees that he has fallen deeper than ever before, how the dear mother's heart only loves him more intensely through all the wretchedness! Scripture says, *"Because he laid down his life for us: and we ought to lay down our lives for the brethren"* (1 John 3:16). The Holy Spirit comes as a spirit of love. If you want to know the joy of the Holy Spirit and want Him to lead you into the rest of God and keep you there, beware, above everything on earth or in hell, of being unloving. One sharp word to your brother or sister brings a cloud upon you without your knowing it. People are so accustomed to talking just as they like about each other that they say nasty, unkind, and unloving things. Then they wonder why things go wrong.

If there is one thing that grieves God, if there is one thing that hinders the Spirit—for the fruit of the Spirit is love—it is the lack of lovingness. If you want to live in the joy of the Holy Spirit, make your covenant with God. "But," you say, "there is a Christian man who makes me so impatient. He irritates me with his stupidity. And there are those worldly men—how they have tempted me in times past and done me harm! And there is that businessman who is trying to ruin me." Take them all and your own wife and children and every one around you and say, "I understand it: Love is rest, and rest is love. God rests in His love. Love is rest, and rest is love; and where there is no love, the rest must be disturbed." Let us say today, "I see what the joy is; it is the joy of always loving, and it is the joy of losing my own life in love to others."

In connection with humility, someone asks, "What about the text, *'in honour preferring one another'* (Romans 12:10)?" When a soul comes into perfect humility before God, it becomes nothing while God becomes all in all. I am nothing. There is no self to be defended. I have said before God, "I am nothing. It is only Your life and light that shines. The honor is Yours, and nothing may offend me but what is against the glory of my God."

Beloved, are you living in the joy of the Holy Spirit? Come and accept a blessing. Give yourself up to a life of humility in which you are nothing, and a life of love, like Christ's, in which you live only for your fellowmen; for the kingdom of God is the joy of the Holy Spirit.

Consecrated for God's Work

My last thought is that the joy of the Holy Spirit is the joy of working for God. It is the joy of the presence of Jesus, the joy of deliverance from sin, the joy of love for the brethren, and the joy of working for God. Some of us have at times felt what an incomprehensible thing it is that the everlasting God should work through us. And we have said, "Lord, what is this that You, the almighty One, work in me and through me, a vile worm by nature?" It is a mystery that passes knowledge, and yet it is so true. The joy of the Holy Spirit comes when a person gives himself up to the Christlike work of carrying the love of God to men. Let us seek the perishing. Let us live and die for souls. Let us live and die that our fellowmen may be reclaimed and brought back to their God.

There is no delight like hearing the joy-song of a newborn soul. But yes, there is another joy that may be as deep. Even if God does not give me the blessing of hearing the newborn soul sing its song, I may have the joy, the sympathy with Jesus in His rejected life, and the assurance that the Father looks with good pleasure on me. When I think of the thousands of believers in the Christian world and then think of the unsaved world, a cry rises in my heart: "What are we doing?" Ah, we need to be crying to God day and night, "Lord God, wake us up. Lord God, let the Holy Spirit burn within us." Are we the true successors of Jesus Christ? Are we indeed the followers and successors of Christ who went all the way to Calvary to give His blood for men? Do let us remember that the joy of the Holy Spirit is the joy of working for God in Christ. I believe that God has new ways and new leadings and new power for His people, if they will only wait on Him.

But what most of us do is this: We thank God for all He has given, we look at all the ways of working we have, and we say that we will try to do our work better. But if we only had a sense of the need, if we had any sense, by the vision of the Holy Spirit, of the state of the millions around us, I am sure we would fall on our faces before God and say, "God help me do something new. Oh, that every fiber of my being may be taken possession of for this great work with God!" The great need is that all Christians would consecrate themselves wholly to God for His work. May God help us to know what the joy of the Holy Spirit is.

Concluding, I ask again, "Do you believe that it is possible for the Lord Jesus, our Shiloh of whom Jacob prophesied, our Joshua, our glorious King and High Priest, to bring you today into the rest of God?" Remember that word in Hebrews, *"As the Holy Ghost saith, today"* (Hebrews 3:7). Today, summon up courage and take up your ministry, your business, your surroundings, your natural temperament, your home, your life for your remaining days on earth and say, "I do not understand it; I do not know what will come. But one thing I do know,

I do absolutely give everything into the hands of the crucified Lamb of God. He will have me in my entirety." And, beloved, remember that Christ will be to you more than you can think or understand, more than you can ask or desire.

Come, let us cast ourselves into those blessed, loving arms, and let us believe even now that our Joshua leads us into the rest of God. His is the rest in which we are saved from self-care, self-seeking, self-trusting, and self-loving. His is the rest in which we do not think of ourselves, but where He who is almighty and omnipresent is always going to be with us and is always working within us. And let us, when we have done that, claim the promise that, as we have sought first the kingdom and God's righteousness, all things will be added unto us. Beloved, the kingdom of God is within you, and it is righteousness and peace and joy in the Holy Spirit. Come; let us claim it even now in simple, childlike, humble faith.

Chapter Eleven

Triumph of Faith

Chapter Eleven

Triumph of Faith

"And the man believed the word that Jesus had spoken unto him."
—John 4:50

Let me quote from the Gospel According to John, chapter 4:

> *So Jesus came again into Cana of Galilee, where he made the water wine. And there was a certain nobleman, whose son was sick at Capernaum. When he heard that Jesus was come out of Judaea into Galilee, he went unto him, and besought him that he would come down, and heal his son: for he was at the point of death. Then said Jesus unto him, Except ye see signs and wonders, ye will not believe.* (vv. 46–48)

There you have the word "*believe*" for the first time.

> *The nobleman saith unto him, Sir, come down ere my child die. Jesus saith unto him, Go thy way; thy son liveth. And the man believed the word that Jesus had spoken unto him, and he went his way.*
> (John 4:49–50)

There you have that word for the second time.

> *And as he was now going down, his servants met him, and told him, saying, Thy son liveth. Then inquired he of them the hour when he began to amend. And they said unto him, Yesterday at the seventh hour the fever left him. So the father knew that it was at the same hour, in the which Jesus said unto him, Thy son liveth: and himself believed, and his whole house.*
> (vv. 51–53)

There you have an example of faith.

This story has often been used to illustrate the different steps of faith in the spiritual life. It was this usage in a sermon that brought the sainted Canon Battersby into the full enjoyment of rest. He had been a most godly man but had lived a life of failure. The story showed him what it meant to rest on the Word and trust the saving power of Jesus. And from that night on, he was a changed man. He went home to testify of it, and, under God, he was allowed to originate the Keswick Convention.

Three Aspects of Faith

Let me point out to you the three aspects of faith that we have here: first, *faith seeking*; then, *faith finding*; and then, *faith enjoying*. Or, better still: *faith struggling, faith resting,* and *faith triumphing*.

First of all, faith struggling. Here was a man, a nonbeliever prominent in the community, who had heard about Christ. He had a dying son at Capernaum and, in his distress, left his home and walked some six or seven hours away to Cana of Galilee. He had heard of the Prophet, possibly, as one who had made water into wine. He had heard of His other miracles around Capernaum, and he had a certain trust that Jesus would be able to help him. He went to Him, and his prayer was that the Lord would come down to Capernaum and heal his son. Christ said to him, *"Except ye see signs and wonders, ye will not believe."* He saw that the nobleman wanted Him to come and stand beside the child.

This man did not have the faith of the Centurion—*"But speak the word only"* (Matthew 8:8). He did have faith; it was faith that came from hearsay and faith that did, to a certain extent, hope in Christ. But it was not the faith in Christ's power that Christ desired. Still

Christ accepted and met this faith. After the Lord had thus told him what He wished—a faith that could fully trust Him—the nobleman cried the second time, *"Sir, come down ere my child die."* Seeing his earnestness and his trust, Christ said, *"Go thy way; thy son liveth."* And then we read that the nobleman believed. He believed and went his way. He believed the word that Jesus had spoken. In that, he rested and was content. And he went away without having any other pledge than the word of Jesus.

As he was walking homeward, the servants met him to tell him that his son lived. He asked at what hour he began to get better. And when they told him, he knew it was at the very hour that Jesus had been speaking to him. He had at first a faith that was seeking and struggling and searching for blessing. Then he had a faith that accepted the blessing simply as it was contained in the word of Jesus. When Christ said, *"Thy son liveth,"* he was content; he went home and found the blessing—his son restored.

Then came the third step in his faith. He believed with his whole house. That is to say, he not only believed that Christ could do just this one thing—the healing of his son—but he also believed in Christ as his Lord. He gave himself up entirely to be a disciple of Jesus. And not only himself, but his whole house, believed in the Lord.

Hope for the Better Life

Many Christians are like the nobleman. They have heard about a better life. They have met certain individuals whose Christian lives have impressed them and, consequently, have felt that Christ can do wonderful things for a man. Many Christians say in their hearts, "I am sure there is a better life for me to live. How I wish I could be brought to that blessed state!" But they do not have much hope for it. They have read and prayed, but they have found everything to be so difficult. If you ask them, "Do you believe Jesus can help you to live this higher life?", they say, "Yes, He is omnipotent." If you ask, "Do you believe Jesus wishes to do it?", they say, "Yes, I know He is loving." And if you say, "Do you believe that He will do it for you?", they at once say, "I know He is willing, but whether or not He will actually do it for me, I do not know. I am not sure that I am prepared. I do not know if I am mature enough. I do not know if I have enough grace for that." And so they are hungering, struggling, wrestling, and often remain unblessed.

This state of things sometimes goes on for years—they are expecting to see signs and wonders and hoping that God, by a miracle, will make them all right. They are just like the Israelites: They limit the Holy One of Israel. Have you ever noticed that it is the very people whom God has blessed so wonderfully who do this? What did the Israelites say? "God has provided water in the wilderness. But can He provide the table, too? We do not think He can." And so we find believers who say, "Yes, God has done wonders. The whole of redemption is a wonder, and God has done wonders for some whom I know. But will God take one as weak as I and make me entirely right?"

Struggling, wrestling, and seeking are the beginnings of faith in you—a faith that desires and hopes. But it must go on further. And how can that faith grow? Look at the second step. There was the nobleman, and Christ told him these wonderful words: *"Go thy way; thy son liveth."* Then the nobleman simply rested in that word of the living Jesus. He rested in it, without any proof of what he was to get and without one man in the world to encourage him. He went home thinking, "I have received the blessing I sought. I have received life from death for my son. The living Christ promised it to me, and in that I rest." The struggling, seeking faith became a resting faith. The man had entered into rest about his son.

Christ within You

And now, dear believers, this is the one thing God asks you to do. God has said that, in Christ, you have eternal life, the more abundant life. Christ has said to you, *"Because I live, ye shall live also"* (John 14:19). The Word says to us that Christ is our peace, our victory over every enemy, who leads us into the rest of God. These are the words of God, and His message has come to us that Christ can do for us what Moses could not have done. Moses had no Christ to live in him. But you have been told that you can have what Moses had not; you can have a living Christ within you. And are you going to believe that, apart from any experience and apart from any consciousness of strength? If the peace of God is to rule in your heart, the God of peace Himself must be there to do it.

The peace is inseparable from the God. The light of the sun—can I separate light from the sun? Utterly impossible. As long as I have the sun, I have the light. If I lose the sun, I lose the light. Take care! Do not seek the peace of God or the peace of Christ apart from God and Christ. But how does Christ come to me? He comes to me in His precious Word. And just as He said to the nobleman, *"Go thy way; thy son liveth"* (John 4:50), so also Christ comes to me today and says, "Go thy way; thy Savior liveth."

"Lo, I am with you alway" (Matthew 28:20). *"I live, and ye shall live also"* (John 14:19). "I wait to take charge of your whole life. Will you let Me do this? Trust to Me all that is evil and feeble, your whole sinful and perverse nature; give it up to Me. That dying, sin-sick soul—give it up to Me, and I will take care of it."

Will you not listen and hear Him speak to your soul? "Child, go forward into all the circumstances of life that have tempted you, into all the difficulties that threaten you." Your soul lives with the life of God. Your soul lives in the power of God. Your soul lives in Christ Jesus. Will you not, like the nobleman, take the simple step of faith and believe the word Jesus has spoken? Will you not say, "Lord Jesus, You have spoken. I can rest on Your Word. I have seen that Christ is willing to be more to me than I ever knew. I have seen that Christ is willing to be my life in the most actual and intense meaning of the word." All that we know about the Holy Spirit sums itself up in this one thing: The Holy Spirit comes to make Christ an actual, indwelling, always-abiding Savior.

God's Fulfilled Promise

Last comes the triumphant faith. The man went home firmly believing in the promise. He had only one promise, but he held it fast. When God gives me a promise, He is just as near to me as when He fulfills it. That is a great comfort. When I have the promise, I also have the pledge of the fulfillment. But the whole heart of God is in His promise, just as much as in the fulfillment of it. Sometimes God, the Promiser, is more precious because I am compelled to cling more to Him, to come closer to Him, to live by simple faith, and to adore His love. Do not think that living upon a promise is a hard life. It means living upon the everlasting God. Who is going to say that is hard? It means living upon the crucified, the loving Christ. Be ashamed to say that is a difficult thing; it is a blessed thing.

The nobleman went home and found the child living. And what happened then? Two things. First, he gave up his whole life to be a believer in Jesus. If there had been a division among the people of Capernaum and thousands of them had hated Christ, this man would still have stood on Christ's side; he believed in the Lord. This is what must take place with us. Let us go forward with our trust in the living Christ, knowing that He will keep us. Then we will receive grace to carry the life of Christ into our whole conduct, into all our walk and conversation. The faith that rests in Jesus is the faith that trusts all to Him, with all we have.

Do we not read that when God had finished His work and rested, it was only to begin new work? Yes, the great work was to be carried on—watching over and ruling His world and His church. And is it not so with the Lord Jesus? When He had finished His work, He sat upon the throne to do His work of perfecting the body of Christ, through the Holy Spirit. And now the Holy Spirit is carrying on that blessed work, teaching us to rest in Christ and, in the strength of that rest, to go on—to cover our whole life with the power, the obedience, the will, and the likeness of the Lord Jesus. The nobleman gave up his whole life to be a believer in Christ. And from that day forward, it was a believer in Jesus who walked about the streets of Capernaum—a man who could not only say, "Once He helped me," but also, "I believe in Him with my whole life." Let that be so with us everywhere. Let Christ be the one object of our trust.

One more thought—the nobleman believed with his whole house. That was triumphant faith. He took up his position as a believer in Christ. Then he gathered his wife, his children, and his servants all together and laid them at the feet of Christ. If you want power in your own house, if you want power in your Bible class, if you want power in your social circle, if you want power in the nation, and if you want power in the church of Christ, see where it begins. Come into contact with Jesus in this rest of faith that accepts His life fully, that trusts Him fully—and the power to overcome the world will come by faith; to bless others, by faith; to live a life to the glory of God, by faith. Go your way; your soul lives, for it is Jesus Christ who lives within you. Go your way. Do not be trembling and fearful, but rest in the Word and the power of the Son of God. *"Lo, I am with you alway"* (Matthew 28:20). Go your way, with your heart open to welcome Him and believing that He has come in.

Surely we have not prayed in vain. Christ has listened to the yearnings of our hearts and has entered in. Let us go our way quietly, restfully, full of praise, joy, and trust, ever hearing the words of our Master, *"Go thy way; thy soul liveth."* Let us say, "I have trusted Christ to reveal His abundant life in my soul. By His grace I will wait upon Him to fulfill His promise." Amen.

Chapter Twelve

The Source of Power in Prayer

Chapter Twelve

The Source of Power in Prayer

"Likewise the Spirit also helpeth our infirmities: for we know not what we should pray for as we ought: but the Spirit itself maketh intercession for us with groanings which cannot be uttered. And he that searcheth the hearts knoweth what is the mind of the Spirit, because he maketh intercession for the saints according to the will of God."
—Romans 8:26–27

Here we have the teaching of God regarding the help the Holy Spirit will give us in prayer. The first half of this chapter is very important in reference to the teaching of God's Word regarding the Spirit.

In Romans 6, we read about being dead to sin and alive to God. In Romans 7, we read about being dead to the law and married to Christ, as well as the inability of the unregenerate man to do God's will. This is only a preparation to show us how helpless we are. And then, in the eighth chapter, comes the blessed work of the Spirit, expressed chiefly in the following words: *"The Spirit of life in Christ Jesus hath made me free from the law of sin and death"* (Romans 8:2). The Spirit makes us free from the power of sin and teaches and leads us so that we walk after the Spirit.

In our inner disposition we may become spiritually minded and enabled to mortify the deeds of the body. The Holy Spirit helps our infirmities. Prayer is the most necessary thing in the spiritual life. Yet we do not know how to pray nor what to pray for as we ought. The Spirit, Paul told us, prays with unutterable groanings. And again he told us that we ourselves often do not know what the Spirit is doing within us, but there is one God who searches the heart. Words often reveal my thoughts and my wishes but not what is deep in my heart. God comes and searches my heart. And deep down, hidden—what I cannot see and what was to me an unutterable longing—God is able to find.

Dependence on God in Prayer

Powerful prayer! The confession of ignorance! Friends, I am often afraid for myself as a minister that I pray too easily. I have been praying for these forty or fifty years and it becomes, as far as man is concerned, an easy thing to pray. We all have been taught to pray, and when we are called upon, we can pray. But it gets far too easy, and I am afraid we think we are praying often when there is little real prayer. Now if we are to have the praying of the Holy Spirit in us, one thing is necessary: We must begin by feeling, "I cannot pray." When a man breaks down and cannot pray, when there is a fire burning in his heart and a burden resting upon him, something is drawing him to God. "I know not what to pray"—oh, blessed ignorance! We are not ignorant enough.

Abraham went out not knowing where he went. There was an element of ignorance and also of faith in his venture. Jesus essentially said to His disciples, when they came with their prayer for the throne, "You know not what you ask." Paul said, *"The things of God knoweth no man, but the Spirit of God"* (1 Corinthians 2:11). You say, "If I am not to pray the old prayers I learned from my mother or from my Sunday school teacher or from my experience yesterday and the day before, what am I to pray?" I answer, pray new prayers; rise higher into the riches of God. You must begin to feel your ignorance. You know what we think of a student who goes to college fancying he knows everything. He will not learn much.

Sir Isaac Newton said, "I do not know what I may appear to the world; but to myself I seem to have been only like a boy playing on the seashore and diverting myself in now and then finding a smoother pebble or a prettier shell than ordinary, whilst the great ocean of truth lay all undiscovered before me." When I see a man who cannot pray glibly and smoothly and readily, I say that is a mark of the Holy Spirit. When he begins, in his prayers, to say, "O God, I want more. I want to be led in deeper. I have prayed for the unsaved, but I want to feel the burden of the nonbelievers in a new way," it is an indication of the presence of the Holy Spirit. I tell you, beloved, if you will take time and let God lay the burden of the unsaved heavier upon you until you begin to feel, "I have never prayed," it will be the most blessed thing in your life.

And so, with regard to the church, we want to take up our position as members of the church of Christ in this land; and as belonging to that great body, we want to say, "Lord God, is there nothing that can be done to bless the church of this land and to revive it and bring it out of its worldliness and out of its feebleness?" We may confer together and conclude faithlessly, "No, we do not know what is to be done. We have no influence or power over all these ministers and their churches." But on the other hand, how blessed to come to God and say, "Lord, we know not what to ask. You know what to grant."

The Holy Spirit could pray one hundredfold more in us if we were only conscious of our ignorance, because we would then feel our dependence upon Him. May God teach us our ignorance in prayer and our helplessness. May God bring us to say, "Lord, we cannot pray; we do not know what prayer is." Of course some of us do know, in a measure, what prayer is. And we may thank God for what He has been to us in answer to prayer; but oh, it is only a little beginning compared to what the Holy Spirit of God teaches.

Phases of Prayer

Our ignorance is the first phase of prayer: *"We know not what we should pray for as we ought: but the Spirit itself maketh intercession for us with groanings which cannot be uttered"* (Romans 8:26). We often hear about the work of God the Father, the Son, and the Holy Spirit in working out and completing the great redemption. And we know that when God worked in the Creation of the world, He was not weary. Yet we read that wonderful expression in the book of Exodus about the Sabbath day, that God *"rested, and was refreshed"* (Exodus 31:17). He was refreshed; the Sabbath day was a refreshment to Him. God had to work; and Christ had to work, and now the Holy Spirit works. His secret working place—the place where all work must begin—is in the heart where He comes to teach a man how to pray. When a man begins to acquire an insight into that which is needed and that which is promised and that which God waits to perform, he feels it to be beyond his conception. Then is the time he will be ready to say, "I cannot limit the Holy One of Israel by my thoughts. I give myself up in the faith that the Holy Spirit can be praying for me with groanings, with longings, that cannot be expressed." Apply that to your prayers.

Then there is the phase of *worship,* when a man bows down to adore the great God. We do not take time to worship. We need secret worship to get ourselves face-to-face with the everlasting God, that He may overshadow us and cover us and fill us with His love and His glory. It is the Holy Spirit who can work in us such a yearning that we will give up our pleasures, and even part of our business, to spend more time with our God.

The next phase of prayer is *fellowship.* In prayer there is not only the worship of a king, but also the fellowship as a child with God. Christians spend far too little time in fellowship. They think prayer is just coming to God with their petitions. If Christ is to make me what I am to be, I must tarry in fellowship with God. If God is to let His love enter in and shine and burn through my heart, I must take time to be with Him. The blacksmith puts his rod of iron into the fire. If he leaves it there for only a short amount of time, it does not become red hot. He may take it out to do something with it and, after a time, put it back again for a few minutes, but this time it does not become red hot either. In the course of the day, he may put the rod into the fire a great many times and leave it there for two or three minutes each time. But it never becomes thoroughly heated. If he takes his time and leaves the rod in the fire for ten or fifteen minutes, the whole iron will become red-hot from the fire's heat.

So if we are to have the fire of God's holiness and love and power, we must spend more time with God in fellowship. That was what gave men like Abraham and Moses their strength. They were men who were separated for fellowship with God, and the living God made them strong. Oh, if we only realized what prayer can do!

Another important phase of prayer is *intercession.* What a work God has initiated for those who are His priests or intercessors! We find a wonderful expression in the prophecy of Isaiah; God said, *"Let him take hold of my strength"* (Isaiah 27:5), and again, *"There is none that calleth upon thy name, that stirreth up himself to take hold of thee"* (Isaiah 64:7). In other passages God referred to the intercessors for Israel. Have you ever taken hold of God? Thank God, some of us have. But friends, representatives of the church of Christ in the world, if God were to show us how much there is of intense prayer for a revival through the church, how much of sincere confession of the sins of the church, how much of pleading with God and giving Him no rest until He makes Jerusalem a glory in the earth, I think we would all be ashamed. We need to give up our hearts to the Holy Spirit, that He may pray for us and in us with groanings that cannot be uttered.

What must I do to have this Holy Spirit within me? The Spirit wants time and room in my heart. He wants my whole being. He wants all my interest and influence to go out for the honor and the glory of God. He wants me to give myself up. Beloved friend, you cannot imagine what you could accomplish if you would only give yourself up to intercession. It is a work that a sick one, lying on a bed year by year, may do in power. It is a work that a poor one, who has hardly a penny to give to missions, can do day by day. It is a work that a young girl, who is in her father's house helping with the housework, can do minute by minute in the Holy Spirit.

People often ask, "What does the church of our day do to reach the masses?" They ask, though they ask it in fear for they feel so helpless, "What can we do to fight the materialism and infidelity in places like London and Berlin and New York and Paris?" We have given it up as hopeless. Ah, if men and women could be called out to band themselves together to take hold of God! I am not speaking of any prayer group or any prayer time statedly set apart. But if the Spirit could find men and women who would give up their lives to cry to God, the Spirit would most surely come. It is not selfish, mere happiness that we seek when we talk about the peace, rest, and blessing Christ can give. God wants us; Christ wants us because He has to do a work. The work of Calvary is to be done in our hearts, and we are to sacrifice our lives to pleading with God for men. Oh, let us yield ourselves day by day and ask God that it may please Him to let His Holy Spirit work in us.

Open Your Heart in Repentance

Then comes the last thought: God Himself comes to look with complacency upon the attitude of His child. Perhaps that poor man does not know how to pray. Perhaps he is ashamed of his prayers. So much the better. Perhaps he feels burdened and restless; but God hears. God discovers what is the mind of the Spirit and will answer. Oh, think of this wonderful mystery: God the Father on the throne ready to grant us His blessings according to the riches of His glory; Christ the almighty High Priest pleading day and night. His whole person is one intercession, and He pleads to the Father, without ceasing, "Bless Your church." And the answer comes from the Father to the Son and from the Son down to the church. And if it does not reach us, it is because our hearts are closed.

Let us open and enlarge our hearts and say to God, "Oh, that I might be a priest, to enter God's presence continually and to take hold of God and to bring down a blessing to my perishing fellowmen!" God longs to find the intercession of Jesus reflected in the hearts of His children; and where He finds it, it is a delight. And he who searches the heart knows the mind of the Spirit, because he prays for the saints according to the will of God. Someone has spoken of those words, *"for the saints,"* as meaning the spirit of praise in the believer for the saints throughout the world. God's Word continually calls us to pray for all and not to be content with ourselves.

Think about the hundreds of church members in this land—many unconverted, many recently converted—who are yet worldly and careless. Think of the thousands of nominal Christians—Christians in name—robbing God! Can we be happy? If we bear the burden of souls, can we have peace and joy? God gives you peace and joy with no other object than to be strong and bear the burden of souls in the joy of Christ's salvation.

We should not say, "I am trying to be as holy as I can. What do I have to do with those worldly people about me?" If there is a terrible disease in my hand, my body cannot say, "I have nothing to do with it." When the people had sinned, Ezra tore his garments, bowed in the dust, and made confession. He repented on the part of the people. And Nehemiah, when the nation had sinned, made confession and cast himself before God, deploring their disobedience to the God of their fathers.

Daniel did the very same thing. Do you think that we as believers do not have a great work to do? Suppose we were each without a single sin; could we then make confession? Look at Christ, without sin! He went down into the waters of baptism with sinners. He made Himself one with them.

God has spoken to us to ask us if we realize what we are. He now asks us whether we belong to the church of this land, whether we have borne the burden of sin around us. Let us go to God; and may He, by the Holy Spirit, fill our hearts with unutterable sorrow at the state of the church. And may God give us grace to mourn before Him. And when we begin to confess the sins of the church, we will begin to feel our own sins as never before. In five of the Epistles to the seven churches in Asia, the keynote was "Repent." There was to be no thought of overcoming and receiving a blessing unless they repented. Let us, on behalf of the church of Christ, repent; and God will give us courage to feel that He will revive His work.

Chapter Thirteen

That God May Be All in All

Chapter Thirteen

That God May Be All in All

"Then cometh the end, when he shall have delivered up the kingdom to God, even the Father; when he shall have put down all rule and all authority and power. For he must reign, till he hath put all enemies under his feet. The last enemy that shall be destroyed is death. For he hath put all things under his feet. But when he saith all things are put under him, it is manifest that he is excepted, which did put all things under him. And when all things shall be subdued unto him, then shall the Son also himself be subject unto him that put all things under him, that God may be all in all."

—1 Corinthians 15:24–28

This will be the grand conclusion of the great drama of the world's history and of Christ's redemption. There will come a day—the glory is such we can form no concept of it, the mystery so deep we cannot realize it—when the Son will deliver up the kingdom that the Father gave Him, that He won with His blood, and that He has established and perfected from the throne of His glory. *"He shall have delivered up the kingdom to God, even the Father."* The Son Himself will be subject also unto the Father, *"that God may be all in all."*

I cannot understand it—the ever blessed Son, equal with God from eternity and through eternity, will be subjected unto the Father. And in some way utterly beyond our comprehension, it will then be made manifest, as never before, that God is all in all. It is this that Christ has been working for. It is this that He is working for today in us. It is this that He thought worthwhile to give His blood for. It is this that His heart is longing for in each of us. This is the very essence and glory of Christianity, *"that God may be all in all."*

Everything Subject to Christ

And now, if this is what fills the heart of Christ—if this expresses the one end of the work of Christ—then, if I want to have the spirit of Christ in me, the motto of my life must be this: everything made subject to and swallowed up in Him, *"that God may be all in all."* What a triumph it would be if the church were really fighting with that banner floating over her! What a life ours could be if that were truly our banner! To serve God fully, wholly, only—to have Him all in all! How it would dignify, enlarge, and stimulate our whole being! I am working, I am fighting, *"that God may be all in all,"* that the day of glory may be hastened. I am praying, and the Holy Spirit makes His wrestling in me with unutterable longing, *"that God may be all in all."*

If only we Christians realized what a grand cause we are working and praying for. If only we had some concept of the kingdom we are partakers of and of the manifestation of God we are preparing for. To illustrate what a grand thing it is to belong to the kingdom of God and to the glorious church of Christ on earth, John McNeil, the Scottish evangelist, told a story of when he was twelve years old. He was working on a railway line and earning the grand wages of six shillings a week. He used to go home to his mother and sisters, who thought no end of their little Johnnie, and delight them by telling of the position he had. He would say with great pride, "Oh, our company, it has so many thousands of pounds passing through its hands every year; it carries so many hundreds of thousands of passengers every year; and it has so many miles of railway and so many engines and carriages and so many thousands in its employ!" And his mother and sisters had great pride in him because he was a partner in such an important business.

Christians, if only we would rouse ourselves to believe that we belong to the kingdom that Christ is preparing to deliver up to the Father, *"that God may be all in all."* Then how the glory would fill our hearts and expel everything mean, low, and earthly! How we should be borne along in this blessed faith! I am living for this: that Christ may have the kingdom to deliver to the Father. I will one day see Him made subject to the Father, and then God will be all in all. I am living for Him, and I will be there not only as a witness, but I will have a part in it all. The kingdom delivered up, the Son made subject, and God all in all! I will have a part in it and, in adoring worship, share the glory and the blessedness. Let us take this home to our hearts, that it may rule in our lives—this one thought, this one faith, this one aim, this one joy: Christ lived and died and reigns. I live and die and, in His power, I reign, only for this one thing: *"That God may be all in all."* Let Him possess each one of our hearts and lives.

Give God First Place

How can God possess my whole heart and life? It is a serious question to which I wish to give you a few simple answers. I say, first of all, allow God to take His place in your heart and life. Luther often said to people, when they come troubling him about difficulties, "Do let God be God." Oh, give God His place. And what is that place? *"That God may be all in all."* Let God be all in all every day, from morning to evening. God to rule, and I to obey.

Ah, the blessedness of saying, "God and I!" What a privilege that I have such a partner! God first and then I! And yet there might be a secret self-exaltation in associating God with myself. And I find in the Bible a more precious word still. It is, "God and not I." It is not, "God first, and I second." God is all, and I am nothing. Paul said, *"I laboured more abundantly than they all: yet not I, but the grace of God which was with me"* (1 Corinthians 15:10). Let us try to give God His place—begin in our closet, in our worship, in our prayer. The power of prayer depends almost entirely upon our understanding of the One with whom we speak. It is of the greatest consequence, if we only have a half hour to pray, that we take time to get a sight of this great God, in His power, in His love, in His nearness, just waiting to bless us. This is of far more consequence than spending the whole half hour in pouring out numerous petitions and pleading numerous promises. The great thing is to feel that we are putting our supplications into the bosom of omnipotent love.

Before and above everything, let us take time before we pray to realize the glory and presence of God. Give God His place in every prayer. I say, allow God to have His place. I cannot give God His place on the throne until I realize what that place is. It is God who will increasingly reveal Himself and the place He holds. How do I know anything about the sun? Because the sun shines, and in its light I see what the sun is. The sun is its own evidence. No philosopher could have told me about the sun if the sun did not shine. No power of meditation and thought can grasp the presence of God. Be quiet and trusting and resting, and the everlasting God will shine into your heart and will reveal Himself. And then, just as naturally as I enjoy the light of the sun on the pages of a book because the light shines on the words, will God reveal Himself to the waiting soul. He will make His presence a reality.

God will take His place as God in the presence of His child so that the chief thing in the child's heart will be: "God is here. God makes Himself known." Beloved, is this not what you long for—that God will take a place He has never had? That God will come to you in a nearness you have never felt yet? And above all, that God will come to you in an abiding and unbroken fellowship? God is able to take His place before you all day. I repeat what I have referred to before, because God taught me a lesson by it. God made the light of the sun so soft, sweet, bright, universal, and unceasing, that it never costs me a minute's trouble to enjoy it. Even more real than the light shining upon me, the nearness of my God can be revealed to me as my abiding portion. Let us all pray *"that God may be all in all"* in our everyday lives.

See God in Everything

"That God may be all in all," I must not only allow Him to take His place; but I must also accept His will in everything. I must accept His will in every providence. Whether it is a Judas who betrays or a Pilate in his indifference who gives me up to the enemy—whatever the trouble, temptation, vexation, or worry, I must see God in it and accept it as God's will for me. It is not God's will that men should do wrong, but it is God's will that they should be in circumstances of trial. There is never a trial that comes to us that is not God's will for us. And, if we learn to see God in it, then we bid it welcome.

Suppose in South Africa there is a woman whose husband has gone on a long journey into the interior. He is to be away from all posts for months. The wife is anxious to receive news. She has had no letter from him in weeks. One day, as she stands in her door, there comes a great African tribesman. He is frightful in appearance and carries his spears and shield. The woman is alarmed and rushes into the house and closes the door. He comes and knocks at the door, and she is in terror. She sends her servant, who comes back and says, "The man says he must see you." She goes, full of fear. He takes out an old newspaper. He has come a month's journey on foot from her husband, and inside the dirty newspaper is a letter from her husband, telling her of his welfare. How the wife delights in that letter! She forgets the face that has terrified her. And now, as weeks are passing away again, she begins to long for that messenger! After a long time he comes again. And this time she rushes out to meet him because he is the messenger who comes from her beloved husband. She knows that he is the bearer of a message of love.

Beloved, have you learned to look at tribulation and vexation and disappointment as this messenger with a spear in his hand, coming straight from Jesus? Have you learned to say, "There is never a trouble and never a hurt by which my heart is touched or even pierced, except that which comes from Jesus and brings a message of love"? Learn to say, "I welcome every trial, for it comes from God." If you want God to be all in all, you must see and meet God in every providence. Oh, learn to accept God's will in everything! Come; learn to say of every trial, without exception, "It is my Father who sent it. I accept it as His messenger." Remember, nothing in earth or hell can separate you from God.

Trust God's Power

If God is to be all and all in your heart and life, I say not only to allow Him to take His place, and accept all His will, but also to trust in His power. Dear friends, it is *"God which worketh both in you to will and to do of his good pleasure"* (Philippians 2:13). It is *"the God of peace,"* according to another passage, that can *"make you perfect in every good work to do His will, working in you that which is wellpleasing in his sight"* (Hebrews 13:20–21). You complain of weakness, of feebleness, of emptiness. Never mind; that is what you are made for: to be an emptied vessel in which God can put His fullness and His strength. Do learn the lesson. I know it is not easy. Long after Paul had been an apostle, the Lord Jesus had to come in a very special way to teach him to say, *"Most gladly therefore will I rather glory in my infirmities"* (2 Corinthians 12:9).

Paul was in danger of being exalted because of his revelations from heaven. And Jesus sent him a thorn in the flesh—yes, Jesus sent it—to buffet him. Paul prayed and struggled and wanted to get rid of it. And Jesus came to him, saying essentially, "It is My doing that you may not be free from that. You need it. I will bless you wonderfully in it." (See 2 Corinthians 12.) Paul's life was changed from that moment in this one respect; and Paul said,

> *And he said unto me, My grace is sufficient for thee: for my strength is made perfect in weakness. Most gladly therefore will I rather glory in my infirmities....for when I am weak, then am I strong.*
> (2 Corinthians 12:9–10)

Do you indeed desire God to be all in all? Learn to glory in your weakness. Take time to say every day as you bow before God, "The almighty power of God that works in the sun, the moon, the stars, and the flowers is working in me. It is as sure as I live. The almighty power of God is working in me. I only need to get down and be quiet. I need to be more submissive and surrendered to His will. I need to be more trustful and to allow God to do with me what He will."

Give God His way with you; let God work, and He will work mightily. The deepest quietness has often been proven to be the inspiration for the highest action. It has been seen in the experience of many of God's saints, and it is just the experience we need—that in the quietness of surrender and faith, God's working has been made manifest.

Give Everything to God

Fourth, if God is to be all in all, Christians must sacrifice everything for His kingdom and glory. *"That God may be all in all."* This is such a noble, glorious, holy aim that Christ said, "For this I will give My life. For this I will give My all, even to the death of the cross. For this I will give Myself." If it was worth that to Christ, is it worth less to you? If one had asked Jesus of Nazareth, "Why is it that You have a body? What is to You the highest use of the body?", He would have said, "The use and the glory of My body is that I can give it as a sacrifice to God. That is everything." What is the use of having a mind or money or children? That I can give them to

God; for God must be all in all in everything. I pray that God will give us such a sight of His kingdom and His glory that everything else may disappear. Then, if you had ten thousand lives, you would say, "This is the beauty and the worth of life: *'That God may be all in all'* to me and that I may prove to men that God is more than everything. Life is only worth living as it is given to God to fill."

Do let us sacrifice everything for His kingdom and glory. Begin to live day by day with the prayer, "My God, I am given up to You. Be my all in all." You say, "Am I able to realize that?" Yes, in this way: Let the Holy Spirit dwell in you; let the Holy Spirit burn in you as a fire. Let Him burn in you with unutterable groanings, crying unto God Himself to reveal His presence and His will in you. In Romans 8, Paul spoke about the groanings of the whole creation. And what is the whole creation groaning for? For the redemption, the glorious liberty of the children of God. And I am persuaded that was what Paul meant when he spoke of the groanings of the Holy Spirit—the unutterable groanings for the coming time of glory when God should be all in all. Christians, sacrifice your time, your interests, and your heart's best powers in praying, desiring, and crying that *"God may be all in all."*

Wait Continually on God

And last, if God is to be all in all, wait continually on Him all day long. My first point had reference to giving God His place. But I want to bring this out more pointedly in conclusion. Wait continually on God all day. If you are to do that, you must always live in His presence. That is what we have been redeemed for. We read in the epistle to the Hebrews, *"Draw nigh unto God"* (Hebrews 7:19). We also read,

> *Which hope we have as an anchor of the soul, both sure and stedfast, and which entereth into that within the veil; whither the forerunner is for us entered, even Jesus, made an high priest for ever.*
> (Hebrews 6:19–20)

The Father never hides His face from His child. Sin hides it, unbelief hides it; but the Father lets His love shine continually on the face of His children. The sun is shining day and night. Your sun will never go down. Begin to seek this. Come and live in the presence of God. There is indeed an abiding place in His presence, in the secret of His pavilion, of which someone has sung very beautifully:

With me, wheresoe'er I wander,
    That great Presence goes;
That unutterable gladness,

Undisturbed repose.
Everywhere, the blessed stillness
Of that Holy Place;
Stillness of the love that worships,
Dumb before His face.

This is the portion of those to whom the prayer is granted—

One thing have I desired of the L*ORD, that will I seek after; that I may dwell in the house of the* L*ORD all the days of my life, to behold the beauty of the* L*ORD, and to inquire in his temple....in the secret of his tabernacle shall he hide me; he shall set me up upon a rock.* (Psalm 27:4–5)

God Himself will take you up and will keep you there so that all your work will be done in God. Beloved, wait continually upon God. You cannot do this unless you are in His presence. You must live in His presence. Then the blessed habit of waiting upon God will be learned. The difficulty in getting to the point of real waiting upon God is that most Christians have not sought to realize the nearness of God, to give God the first place. But let us strive after this. Let us trust God to give it to us by His grace. Let us wait on God all the day.

"My eyes," one says, "are ever toward you." Wait upon God for guidance, and God will lead you up into new power for His service, into new gladness in His fellowship. He will lead you out into a larger trust in Him. He will prepare you to expect new things from Him. Beloved, there is no knowing what God will do for a man who is utterly given up to Him. Praise His name! Let each one of us say, "May my life be to live and die, to labor and to pray continually, for this one thing: that in me, around me, in the church, and throughout the world, *'God may be all in all.'*"

A little seed is the beginning of a great tree. A mustard seed becomes a tree in which the birds of the air can nestle. That great day of which the text speaks—when Christ Himself will be subject to the Father and will deliver up the kingdom to the Father, and God will be all in all—that is the great tree of the kingdom of God reaching its perfect consummation and glory. Oh, let us take the seed of that glory into our hearts. And let us bow in lowly surrender and submission and say, "Amen, Lord, let it be: My one thought in life is to speak and to work, to pray and to exist only that others may be brought to know Him, too. Let this be my life: to yield myself to the unutterable yearnings of the Holy Spirit, that I may not rest, but ever keep my eyes on that day—the day of glory—when, in every deed, *God will be all in all.*"

God help every one of us. God help us all to yield ourselves to Him and to Christ and to make it our daily life, for His name's sake. Amen.

About the Author

About the Author

Andrew Murray (1828-1917)

Andrew Murray was an amazingly prolific Christian writer. He lived and ministered as both a pastor and author in the towns and villages of South Africa. Some of Murray's earliest works were written to provide nurture and guidance to Christians, whether young or old in the faith; they were actually an extension of his pastoral work. Once books such as *Abide in Christ, Like Christ,* and *With Christ in the School of Prayer* were written, Murray became widely known, and new books from his pen were awaited with great eagerness throughout the world.

He wrote to give daily practical help to many of the people in his congregation who lived out in the farming communities and could come into town for church services only on rare occasions. As he wrote these books of instruction, Murray adopted the practice of placing many of his more devotional books into thirty-one separate readings to correspond with the days of the month.

At the age of seventy-eight, Murray resigned from the pastorate and devoted most of his time to his manuscripts. He continued to write profusely, moving from one book to the next with an intensity of purpose and a zeal that few men of God have ever equaled. He often said of himself, rather humorously, that he was like a hen about to hatch an egg; he was restless and unhappy until he got the burden of the message off his mind.

During these later years, after hearing of pocket-sized paperbacks, Andrew Murray immediately began to write books to be published in that fashion. He thought it was a splendid way to have the teachings of the Christian life at your fingertips, where they could be carried around and read at any time of the day.

One source has said of Andrew Murray that his prolific style possesses the strength and eloquence that are born of deep earnestness and a sense of the solemnity of the issues of the Christian life. Nearly every page reveals an intensity of purpose and appeal that stirs men to the depths of their souls. Murray moves the emotions, searches the conscience, and reveals the sins and shortcomings of many of us with a love and hope born out of an intimate knowledge of the mercy and faithfulness of God.

For Andrew Murray, prayer was considered our personal home base from which we live our Christian lives and extend ourselves to others. During his later years, the vital necessity of unceasing prayer in the spiritual life came to the forefront of Andrew Murray's teachings. It was then that he revealed the secret treasures of his heart concerning a life of persistent and believing prayer.

Countless people the world over have hailed Andrew Murray as their spiritual father and given credit for much of their Christian growth to the influence of his priceless devotional books.

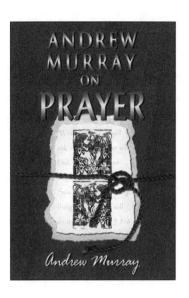

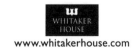

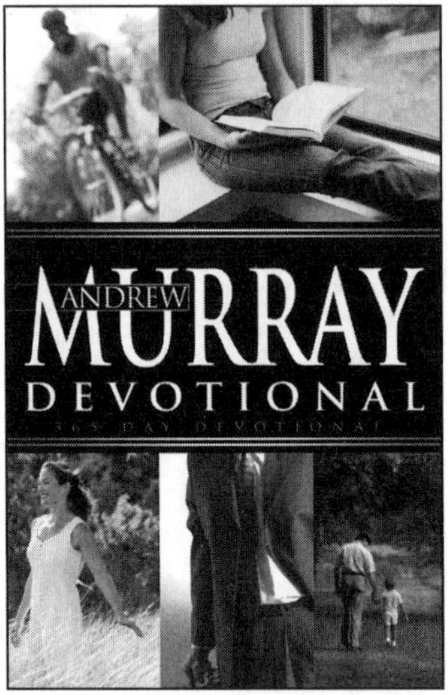

Andrew Murray Devotional

Andrew Murray

These uplifting messages for each day of the year will comfort and refresh you in your walk with God. Spending time with God daily will bring a new joy and peace into your life. As you daily explore these truths gleaned from Andrew Murray's writings, you will connect with God's glorious power and see impossibilities turn into realities. Your prayer life will be transformed. You will experience the joy of seeing powerful results as you minister to others. Don't miss out on the most important part of the day—your miraculous, life-changing moments spent with the Creator.

ISBN: 978-0-88368-778-9 • Trade • 400 pages

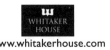

WHITAKER HOUSE
www.whitakerhouse.com